Seven Kinds

Of

Knowledge

A journey of transformation and of becoming what you know!

John T. Muzam

All scriptural quotations, unless otherwise indicated, are taken from the King James Version and New King James Version of the Bible.

Most definitions are derived from the vine's expository dictionary of New Testament words (William Edwy Vine), Strong's Exhaustive Bible Concordance, Thayer's Greek Lexicon, and many others including personal research and inspiration from the author.

Cover designed by: Alexander Bondaruk
Interior design: Henry Igharo
Edited by: Kizito Leacock

John T. Muzam

Kiev – Ukraine
Tel: +380631591470
Email: fatherjohnmuzam@gmail.com
Cameroon:
Tel: (237) 746 296 65
sosemministries@yahoo.com
USA:
Tel: (011) 513 609 9076

ISBN-13: 978-1503361409
ISBN-10:   1503361403

DEDICATION

I dedicate this book to the Holy Spirit!

To my parents Moses Muzam and Endam Margaret; for their unending support and contributions to my life without which I would not have been where I am today. There is no way I can repay them because their investment into my life is an eternal treasure!

I am also grateful to God's generals Pastors Sunday and Bose Adelaja: their lives and ministry are a blessing to me. Pastor Sunday's hard work and its impact on my life are tools that keep me burning the midnight oil in search of knowledge that brings transformation and the ability to maximize time.

ACKNOWLEDGEMENTS

I wish to appreciate the authors who have contributed immensely to my life through their various published materials. Thanks also to those who have contributed their time and effort to make this book a success, namely: Kizito Leacock, Henry Igharo, Antony Waiyaki, Elizabeth Ekakoro, Blessing Imabong Nde, Paul Bokwe, Abam Emmanuel and many others.

A journey of transformation and of becoming what you know!

CONTENTS

FOREWORD

It's an honor to be writing a foreword for Brother John Muzam's book: *7 Kinds Of Knowledge*. This is a relevant book for all times, especially for this information age in which we live. Our time is full of all kinds of information and knowledge, but the basis of all knowledge should be the Scripture. All our other knowledge should be built on the Scripture. Without this, a person would get it wrong in life, despite success in some other areas.

The right knowledge should never be taken for granted. Our lives are reflections of what we did or do with the right knowledge we possess. What we know and do with that knowledge draw the line between us and other individuals. Besides, the depth of a person's knowledge is what determines the distance between him and others in similar circumstances.

This book is very challenging, calling us to desire more of God; to go deeper in Him, to a depth which nominal Christians and unbelievers would consider too deep. The more the truth we know and apply, the freer we become. The right knowledge is power indeed.

The Bible says "without me you cannot bear fruit," this book underlines this, stirring us not to take things for granted but to measure the fruitfulness of our thoughts and deeds.

We can be all God says we are created to be. We can realize all of God's potentials in us if only we are willing and ready to do our part. God created us in such a way that we are like Him – we have our parts to play. Understanding this will explode our mind and world and this will eventually bring us great results. Your imagination, ability and motivation level will progressively increase. However, there is a need to answer this question: will we make it work by doing our own parts with all the available kinds of knowledge we possess or can possess?

Knowledge gives us strength – physically, spiritually, mentally etc. The outcome and results of life depend on us because we have been given absolute will power and delegated authority. The will power that God gave man has the power to make man whatever he decides to be.

This will require sacrifice, labor, some kind of pain, discipline, sweat etc. It will take all this for us to accomplish what God created us for. However, satisfaction comes after sacrifice, favor comes after labor, gain comes after pain, sweet comes after sweat.

This is wisdom and wisdom is the principal thing. However, you cannot have wisdom without knowledge. For wisdom is the application of knowledge. So, definitely apply the knowledge in this book it and you will be blessed with results!

This book is indeed an asset to Christians of all spiritual ages & times. It will make a wonderful and enjoyable Bible study outline.

Remember the more you know Christ who is true knowledge, the more sinless you become.

Happy Reading!

Pastor Bose Adelaja
Snr Pastor; The Embassy of the Blessed
Kingdom of God for All Nations
Kiev –Ukraine

There is no Soldier joining the army who is not carrying a dream or vision of one day becoming a Field Marshall or at least a General, so also in this your walk and work with the Lord God make sure your target or vision is Epignosis and remain diligently focused in pursuing it until our Lord Jesus Christ is fully formed in you according to the prayers of Apostle Paul.

This book you are now glancing through is written in a step by step growth format, based on Biblical knowledge to help you avoid the two major pit falls of most Christians - *where there is no vision* (knowledge), *the people perish* and *my people are destroyed for lack of knowledge.* So follow these laid down steps of needed knowledge and you will make your calling, purpose and election sure; you will never be barren or unfruitful in any area of life and you will never fall or fail in the unfailing name of our Lord Jesus Christ.

Dr. Ovie Osoroh

Pastor, at The International Church;
The Embassy of the Blessed Kingdom of
God for All Nations
Kiev - Ukraine

The fact that someone could write such a book is proof that he has tapped into the various kinds of knowledge revealed in this book. Therefore, this book is its own proof. Selah.

Feed on it, find the gems, and discover the Source of all knowledge.

Kizito Leacock
Editor, Embassy of God Central Church
Birmingham, United Kingdom

PREFACE

Knowledge is actually a treasure that lies within. It can't be seen in a laboratory. Doctors cannot tell how much knowledge you have. It cannot be quantified! It is the most powerful tool that impacts the entire universe. It lies deep within human vessels and only expresses itself when you release your inner man. When you act, speak, write or use any other means of expression, you release knowledge.

Knowledge is everything you need. Knowledge expresses your personality, it determines who you are. No one is born with knowledge, it must be acquired. Knowledge is available to everyone and it is in abundance everywhere. God does not create knowledge every day: He has released knowledge into the atmosphere and it is left for man to tune his brain to the correct frequency of knowledge in order to receive it. Everyone was born with an equal ability to receive knowledge; but why is it that some have more than others? What is knowledge and how many kinds of knowledge really do exist?

When you die, your knowledge dies with you. Only your legacy, the results of your knowledge, is left behind. Its impact may last forever, depending on how effective it was. This book is about to take you through an odyssey of knowledge; thus your life will never be the same again. God bless you as you feed on the pages of this book.

John T. Muzam

Kiev - Ukraine

Chapter 1

What is Knowledge?

In response to the Sadducees' question about resurrection, Jesus said;

"Ye do err, not knowing the scripture nor the power of God"

Matthew 22:29

In other versions, it says we go wrong because we don't know the scriptures; therefore our victory in life is determined by our knowledge of the scriptures. The extent to which we know the scriptures will determine its effect in our lives. The word of God is a picture of our future. Who we are today is a carbon copy of all we know. Knowledge is the vital key that liberates a man or a generation from every satanic or oppressive situation. The difference between our generation and the previous generation is knowledge. Knowledge is the main thing that distinguishes us.

15

The difference between one nation and another is the extent of their knowledge. Knowledge determines who we are and what we do. We have moved from the stone age, to the agricultural age to the technological age etc. The vehicle behind this progression of man through the ages is knowledge.

Knowledge determines our actions, and our actions determine who we become. We become who God says we are only when we actually have the knowledge of who God says we are. Let me make it clear here that the emphasis is not on who God is; for we will hardly know Him completely as humans. Therefore, it is on whether we understand what He says. For what He says makes us know Him. I will explain further; the scripture says;

"My people are destroyed for lack of knowledge"

Hosea 4:6

We are not destroyed because God doesn't want to save us. No, but simply because we lack knowledge. Knowledge determines the greatness of a people, a nation, a community or an environment. Knowledge makes you. You are a product of knowledge. Some say knowledge is information and you are a product of the information you process.

Jesus came to preach deliverance to the captives and the poor. It is the preaching of deliverance that liberated you from your captivity or poverty. Jesus came to proclaim information or knowledge to you. By receiving that knowledge, you receive your deliverance. You become free from poverty, sickness, etc. as a result of your reception of knowledge preached.

"The spirit of the Lord is upon me because He hath anointed me to PREACH the gospel to the poor... to PREACH deliverance to the captive"

Luke 4:18

Deliverance is preached and the gospel is also preached. How it is preached determines how it is received, and that which is received determines the image and the perception the recipient has. For example, the way in which you describe a person to me will determine my understanding of the person and thus my action towards him or her. Your attitude towards God is directly proportional to your knowledge of Him. What you know about Him is actually who He is to you.

Do you see Him as a religious myth, a philosophy or an illusion? The way you see Him will determine your actions, and your actions will determine your results in life. Your actions are simply seeds sown into your life and the results are inevitable. You bear the results of your actions because this world is governed by the law of sowing and reaping.

Your perception of God, a country, a person or a book, is a result of the knowledge you have received regarding that person or thing. If the knowledge was accurately passed to you, then you will have the accurate knowledge of the thing or person. I have come across several Europeans who have never been to Africa, but they have a perceived knowledge of Africa in a dimension in which they believe to be perfectly true. More often than not, they are wrong, yet they tend to stick to their preconceived notion of Africa. This information has usually been conveyed to them through books, media, movies, etc. How well it was passed determines what they know. Therefore, your knowledge of a thing is not often determined by the thing, but by the information you have received about it.

The knowledge you have about God doesn't mean that that is who God is; rather, it is merely how you perceive God. God Himself is aware that man is unable to truly describe Him. He knows that man's knowledge of Him is determined by the information he has of Him. In most cases such information is obtained through the environment or the experiences of man. Moses asked God a peculiar question about His personality:

"And God said unto Moses, I AM THAT I AM: and he said, Thus shall you say unto the children of Israel, I AM has sent me unto you"

Exodus 3:14

Fascinating of course! God did not use anything on earth, beneath the earth or in heavens to identify Himself. There was and is nothing that could describe Him. He simply is: "*I AM that I AM*". Realize that if God wanted to illustrate who He was, He would have used something that could paint an accurate picture of Himself to Moses but there was nothing on planet earth that could accurately describe God. He is simply *I AM*. The knowledge you have about Him is what and who He is to you.

There is no description to explain the personality of God; this is why He is seen as the God of Abraham, the God of Isaac and the God of Jacob. This was a more suitable way for God to describe Himself and help the Israelites to understand His personality.

The Kingdom of God

The Kingdom of God also cannot be explained in words. It can only be known and understood experientially. Have you ever

20

noticed that Jesus would use similes when teaching the kingdom? Jesus would say *"the Kingdom of God is like..."* not: -the kingdom of God is. Our words cannot properly describe the Kingdom.

Again, the Kingdom of heaven is like a merchant seeking beautiful pearls, who when he had found one pearl of great price, went and sold all that he had and bought it.

"Again, the Kingdom of heaven is like a dragnet that was cast into the sea and gathered some of every kind... the Kingdom of heaven is like a householder who brings out of his treasure things new and old"

Matthew 13:44-46,52

The more you have any particular level of knowledge of the Kingdom, the more you yearn for more. Just as it is written in the bible, *"deep calleth unto deep"*. You're never satisfied with the level in which you are. There is always a hunger for the next level of knowledge of God and His Kingdom.

And He said, "The Kingdom of God is as if a man should scatter seed on the ground, and should sleep by night and rise by day, and the seed should sprout and grow, he himself does not know how." Mark 4:26-27

Then He said, "To what shall we liken the Kingdom of God? Or with what parable shall we picture it? It is like a mustard seed which, when it is sown into the ground, is smaller than all the seeds on earth; but when it is sown, it grows up and becomes greater than all herbs, and shoots out large branches, so that the birds of the air may nest under its shade."

"The Kingdom of God is like a man who casts seeds upon the soil"

Mark 4:30-32

Jesus made a habit of using parables or common examples from our natural environment to help us understand the beauty of the Kingdom. It is like a seed: small, but it will expand when it is sown. In the Kingdom, there is growth and it is a necessity. Your growth in knowledge is determined by the information you have. In talking about the Kingdom, Jesus warns us:

"Take heed what you hear. With the same measure you use, it will be measured to you; and to you who hear, more will be given"

Mark 4:24 (NKJV)

What you hear, read or watch determines the knowledge you acquire. The knowledge you have determines the results you will get and the results you get determine your life. There is a direct relationship between what you believe and your knowledge. Your knowledge determines your belief system. Your believe system is cling to your knowledge and thus it determines and shapes your future.

Therefore, I encourage you to define your friends and determine your environment. Create boundaries for yourself, to shape your thoughts and create a perfect lifestyle for yourself. Poverty for example, is not a problem in itself, knowledge or lack thereof is the real problem. The knowledge you have is what has determined the lifestyle you live today. Don't allow cowardice or ignorance to pull you down: associate with people of knowledge – the right kind of knowledge of course.

Many false teachers, philosophers and scientists claim that they can disprove the existence of God. NEVER! This is just an illusion on their part and has no element of truth in it. It violates even the laws of nature. Brethren, even nature can bear witness to you of the undeniable existence of God. Do not believe cowards! The book of Proverbs calls them fools. To be in the company of fools is to become a fool yourself. Truth cannot be denied. The truth is truth and God is willing to prove to you that He is with you. If only you cooperate with the Spirit within you, you will hear the still small voice that would usher you to greatness in life.

Righteousness, Peace and Joy in the Holy Ghost

What therefore is the Kingdom of God? The Kingdom of God is within us and it is righteousness, peace and Joy in the Holy Ghost.

"The Kingdom of God is not meat and drink, but righteousness and peace and joy in the Holy Ghost"

Romans 14:17

Perhaps you need something more to convince you? You need a mystery? No! Do not despise the simplicity of the gospel (2 Cor. 11:3). Let not your mind be troubled from the simplicity that is in Christ. The way you see this is pertinent to the knowledge you have.

Let's continue and I will explain the Kingdom and the knowledge needed to draw this water from within. Remember the Kingdom of God is not in words but in power. Words are limited in that they only paint partial pictures of the Kingdom but experience on the other hand

25

paints a full picture. Power gives us experience. You therefore need knowledge to understand the truth. The right knowledge imparted into your spirit will give you the right experience. The day you receive Christ into your life, the Word was preached and knowledge was imparted and thus you have the experience of a new life, a new creation. It was knowledge that caused you to take a step further to follow Christ. It was a certain knowledge that influenced your action. Our actions are prime factors of the knowledge we possess.

There are different kinds of knowledge in the world. Since we are talking about Godly or biblical knowledge, we are going to examine seven kinds of knowledge found in the New Testament. Remember there are many of them but we are going to study just seven. I pray that the Holy Spirit will help you to have an experience with Him as you study further on the types of knowledge explained in this book. Be assured that your life will never be the same again because you are about to go into an odyssey of discovery that will transform your life. After acquiring this knowledge, the consciousness of it will have a tremendous impact on your life. It will rid you of every doubt and all confusion in life.

If you read the bible superficially, you will see where it talks about knowledge (know, known) in many places and think it refers to the same thing each time. For example, let us look at the few scriptures below using the King James Version of the New Testament.

1. For now we see in a mirror, dimly, but then face to face. Now I know (ginōskō) in part, but then I shall know (epiginōskō) just as I also am known (epiginōskō).   1 Corinthians 13:12

2. And you shall know (ginōskō) the truth, and the truth shall make you free.

3. Yet you have not known (ginōskō) Him, but I know (eidō) Him. And if I say, 'I do not know (eidō) Him,' I shall be a liar like you; but I do know (eidō) Him and keep His word.   John 8:32,55

4. Therefore do not be like them. For your Father knows (eidō) the things you have need of before you ask Him. For after all these things the Gentiles seek. For your heavenly Father knows (eidō) that you need all these things. Matthew 6:8,32

5. You will know (epiginōskō) them by their fruits. Do men gather grapes from thorn bushes or figs from thistles? Matthews 7:16

6. Ever learning and never able to come to the knowledge (epignōsis) of the truth." 2 Timothy 3:7

7. "For if we sin willfully after we have received the knowledge(epignōsis) of the truth, there no longer remains a sacrifice for sins" Hebrews 10:26

All the above verses use the same words: *knowledge, known, know,* but are all communicating something different. The English language is limited in fully expressing the meaning of the words spoken. To fully extract and understand their meanings, we need to go to the original language of those words and the context in which they were used. The fact that the English word is limited as compared to the original one doesn't mean that the Holy Spirit won't help us understand what is said. Of course He will! We live according to the Spirit, not according to the letters, *"for the letter killeth"* (2 Corinthians 3:6)

Definition of Knowledge

Webster's dictionary gives the following definition of knowledge:

1.   The act or state of knowing; clear perception of fact, truth, or duty; certain apprehension; familiar cognizance; cognition.

"Knowledge, which is the highest degree of the speculative faculties, consists in the perception of the truth of affirmative or negative propositions." John Locke.

2.   That which is or may be known; the object of an act of knowing; a cognition; - chiefly used in the plural.

"There is a great difference in the delivery of the mathematics, which are the most abstracted of knowledge." Sir W. Hamilton

3.   That which is gained and preserved by knowing; instruction; acquaintance; enlightenment; learning; scholarship; erudition.

Knowledge puffeth up, but charity edifieth.

4.   That familiarity which is gained by actual experience; practical skill; as a knowledge of life.

Chapter 2

Ginosko Knowledge

The first kind of knowledge we will explore is Ginosko. It is used about 223 times in the King James Version of the Greek Lexicon. It means: "to be taking in knowledge, to come to know, to recognize, to understand or to understand completely."

When using this word in the past tense, it means "to know in the sense of realizing." In the passive voice, it signifies "to become known" as in Philippians 4:5, *"Let your moderation be known unto all men. The Lord is at hand."* It can also be found in Matthew 10:26, *"Fear them not therefore: for there is nothing covered, that shall not be revealed; and hid, that shall not be known."*

Ginosko is also a sense of complete and absolute understanding on God's part as can be seen in John 10:15, *"As the father knoweth me, even so knoweth I the father."* Here Jesus speaks of a full and complete knowledge that the Father has of Him and He of the Father.

Therefore, Ginosko is a complete and absolute knowledge. Let us explore further. Ginosko is also used in 1 Corinthians 3:20, *"And again the Lord knoweth the thoughts of the wise, that they are vain."* When God knows, He knows. He doesn't know partially, He knows in full.

Ginosko frequently indicates the relationship between the person "knowing" and the object "known". In this regard, what is "known" is of value or importance to the one who knows and thus the establishment of the relationship. It is as a result of this knowledge that we are able to establish a relationship with the Creator. I can say that it is the starting point of our Christian faith. It is because you have known him that you decide to start a relationship with Him and welcome Him into your life.

"But if any man loves God, the same is known (ginosko) of him"

1 Corinthians 8:3

"But now after you have known God or rather are known by God"

Galatians 4:9

We see from the scripture above that this kind of knowing suggests approval or carries the meaning of "to be approved". When you know Him, He Himself approves of knowing you. You know God, and God confirms He knows you. The one you know knows you because you know him as well. If not, you would be the only one that knows the other in the "relationship" as the other would not know you. This kind of knowledge demands a mutual relationship.

"Nevertheless the solid foundation of God stands, having this seal, The Lord knows (ginosko) those who are his." and let everyone who names the name of Christ depart from iniquity"

2 Timothy 2:19

"My sheep hear my voice, and I know them. And they follow"

John 10:27

This is a knowing in which the knower and the object know each other. The knower's relationship is approved by the object. God approves us because we know Him. When we say we have ginosko, it implies that we have a relationship with God that has been confirmed and approved by God. This relationship may involve chastisement. God becomes your Father, your Mentor and your Lord. He directs your path and may chastise you when need be.

"You only have I known from among all of the families of mankind: therefore I will hold you accountable for all of your iniquities"

Amos 3:2 (ISV)

"For when the Lord loves he chastens, and scourges every son whom he receives"

Hebrew 12:6

Therefore you will give account for your actions. Remember ginosko refers to those who have established a relationship with the Creator. You submit to His leading through His Spirit that has dwelt in you since the day you established a relationship with Him. Disobedience to His leading simply leads you astray. When He leads you, He leads you in the right direction and your disobedience to His leading implies that you prefer your own direction. The steps of the righteous are ordered by the Lord (Psalms 37:23). You can in some instances disobey His leading and order your own step, thus face the consequences thereof.

The Chastisement of the Lord

Because of this relationship that you have established with him, give Him room to chastise and direct you. The chastisement or scourges of the Lord have nothing to do with that which has been dealt with on the cross. It has nothing to do with sin or the price that has

35

been paid on the cross. It has nothing to do with you when you repent from your acts and follow God's path. God doesn't punish His children. He can't chastise you with sickness, pain, sin, curses etc. These things have been nailed on the cross through His son Jesus. Jesus was chastised for our sake. The chastisement of our peace was upon Him and He nailed them on the cross. It has been nailed there forever and never to be revoked (Isaiah 53:5).

When God chastises His child, He does it with love, as a father corrects his son. You know Jesus came to establish this Father-Son relationship. If you can understand the relationship between a good father and his son, then you'll understand the relationship between you and God as your Father.

A true father will correct, chastise or scourge his son. When the father does so, it is for the son's perfection. You chastise your child not out of anger but out of love. We correct our children so that they wouldn't repeat similar mistakes in the future. The majority of spoilt children are those who were never chastised by their fathers. They were regarded as sweet puppies. The sweet puppies have now become bitter pills to the society. The father needs not to spare the rod, because if he spares the rod, he hates you.

"He who spares the rod hates His son but he who loves him disciplines him promptly"

Proverbs 13:24 (NKJV)

Charles H. Spurgeon, one of England's most influential preachers of the 19th Century known by many as the "prince of preachers" gave a good and fascinating explanation:

"Punishment can never happen to a child of God in the judicial sense, he can never be brought before God as his Judge, as charged with guilt, because that guilt was long ago transferred to the shoulders of Christ, and the punishment was exacted at the hands of his surety. But yet, while the sin cannot be punished, while the Christian cannot be condemned, he can be chastised, while he shall never be arraigned before God's bar as a criminal, and punished for his guilt, yet he now stands in a new relationship—that of a child to his parent: and as a

son he may be chastised on account of sin. Folly is bound up in the heart of all God's children, and the rod of the Father must bring that folly out of them....

There are two dangers against which a person under the chastising hand of God should always be very careful to keep a strict look-out. They are these:"My son despise not thou the chastening of the Lord." That is one. On the other hand: "Neither faint when thou art rebuked of him." Two evils: the one is despising the rod and the other is fainting under it.... The first evil to which the chastened Christian is liable is this: he may despise the hand of God. The second is, that he may faint when he is rebuked. We will begin with the first: "My son despise not thou the chastening of the Lord." This may be done in five ways, and in discussing the subject, I shall propose the remedy for each of these as we pass along.

First, a man may despise the chastening of the Lord when he murmurs at it. Secondly, we despise the chastening of the Lord when we say there is no use in it. There are certain things that happen to us in life, which we immediately set down for a providence. There is a third way in which men despise the chastening of the Lord, that is—we may think it dishonorable to be chastened by God. How many men have thought it to be dishonorable to be persecuted for righteousness sake! Again, in the fourth place, we despise the chastening of the Lord, when we do not earnestly seek to amend by it. Many a man has been corrected by God, and that correction has been in vain. And lastly, we despise the chastening of the Lord when we despise those that God chastens."

This is just a summary; you may go read the entire Charles Spurgeon sermon on this topic. Perhaps you already have it in mind, if God does not chastise or punish us with sickness, poverty, curses etc., then what does He chastise us with? There are many ways in which God chastises His children. He goes further to tell us this:

"My son, despise you not the chastening of the Lord, nor faint when you are rebuked of Him"

Hebrews 12:5

"For whom the Lord loveth He correcteth, even as a father a son in whom he delighteth"

Proverbs 3:12

"Blessed is the man whom thou chastenest o Lord"

Psalms 94:12

"Behold, happy is the man whom the Lord correcteth: therefore despise not the chastening of the Lord almighty"

Job 5:17

Absolute Dependency

Before expatiating further on this, I would like you to note that the Israelites did not bother to cast out the demons we strive to cast out today; though they were opposed by the same satan that we are opposed by today. For, satan has not been redeemed, He has simply been dethroned! Despite what they went through in their walk to the Promise Land, they looked

40

above and complained to the One above. They held Him responsible for all their circumstances. They would either complain or talk against Moses and not to the Devil. Even though, they were well aware that unclean spirits were still on earth, yet they never bothered accusing or blaming the devil.

They were God's people and they had a mindset of absolute awareness of God. Even when they doubted, they knew that there was a God. They created graven images in their eagerness and bid to worship God. They had a longing for that deity on whose supremacy they could have absolute dependence. They didn't bother to cast the devil in any situation; rather they were much more interested in bringing God into their circumstances. While they complained to Moses in Numbers 20:4, ("*Is it because there are no graves in Egypt that you brought us to die in the wilderness? What have you done to us by bringing us out of Egypt?*"), they were still a people who needed an action or response from the sovereign Being. They murmured and complained at the chastisement of the Lord.

"Why have you brought up the congregation of the Lord into the wilderness, that we and our cattle should die there?"

Exodus 20:4

They cried to Moses and Moses turned to God. Who do you cry to when things seem contrary, God or the devil? Like the Israelites we have to believe with absolute truth that we are God's people and the devil has no role in our life. This kind of absolute dependency will cause God to come to your rescue.

Moses turned to God and God's glory fell on Moses to *"speak life into the rock before their eyes."* By so doing, His glory could be made manifest to the people of Israel. God wanted Moses to speak to the rock and not to hit the rock. In disbelief, Moses hit the rock rather than speaking to it and as a result, he was forbidden from entering the Promised Land. There is a reason and purpose for everything under the sun. There is a reason why you are going through what you are going through. It is not because of your sins or your father's sins, but that the glory of the Lord may be made manifest in your life.

When you have this ginosko knowledge of God, you become free from sin to walk in righteousness. God doesn't want you to end there. He wants all men to be saved and to come to the full knowledge (epignosis) of the truth. The knowledge - epignosis, is what we are going to talk about in the last chapter of this book.

After giving so much credit to this type of knowledge we may end up feeling that this is all that is needed to be a child of God; but no! God wants us to come to the full knowledge of Christ (Ephesians 4:13).

Ginosko knowledge is not a guarantee that you have come to the end or that you that will make it to Heaven. Let's read further and we will see the scripture which reveals that many didn't make it even though they had ginosko knowledge of God.

In the first chapter of Romans, God spoke, making Himself known (ginosko) to the people. They knew Him, yet they did not retain Him in this knowledge and as a result they were given to their reprobate mind.

"Because, although they knew (ginosko) God, they did not glorify Him as God, nor were thankful, but became futile in their thoughts, and their foolish hearts were darkened. Professing to be wise, they became fools, and changed the glory of the incorruptible God into an image made like corruptible man—and birds and four-footed animals and creeping things. Therefore God also gave them up to uncleanness, in the lusts of their hearts, to dishonor their bodies among themselves"

Roman 1:21-24

God gave them up to their vile affections; they became homosexuals, committing evil and pursuing after their own desires. What was the cause of all of these?

"And even as they did not like to retain God in their knowledge, God gave them over to a debased mind, to do those things which are not fitting; who, knowing the righteous judgment of God, that those who practice such things are deserving of death, not only do the same but also approve of those who practice them"

Romans 1: 28,32

They knew the law of the Lord. They were aware of the precepts of God, yet they rejected and refused to retain God and to grow in knowledge, as a result they were given up to their vile affections. These events were recorded in the New Testament, they occurred after the death and resurrection of our Lord Jesus Christ. They happened in our dispensation and still continue to happen even to this day. You may find Christians who say *"I don't want to know God more. I just want to know Him a little. I don't want to go deep. Knowing Him this way is already enough for me as it is."* I even met a sister who told me, *"I don't want my husband to be too spiritual. I just want Him to know God and not go deep into it."* How

45

frustrating such statements are! Refusing to go deep is standing at the surface of salvation and standing at the surface is the beginning of frustration.

Such a person is simply suffering from a religious spirit and knows not who she is in Christ. If knowing God deeper is madness, then knowing Him just a little is frustration plus madness. You should not even think of knowing Him a little because you will be in lifelong bondage and you will need grace to be free from it.

Do we really know what Christianity is? Christianity is not a religion; it is a lifestyle that is more superior to any life you can ever imagine. Religiousness keeps us bound to activities that bear no fruit. We should not mistake Christianity for activity. A lot of religious believers are bound to activities that do not lead to growth in their spiritual lives. There was a time that I found myself going to church meetings that have nothing to do with my spiritual growth. I sat under ministrations for hours and days and at the end I asked myself what was the impact of such meetings on my life. Nothing! I mean, I tried to be blessed but the message was cloudy. Some ministers have to be careful how spiritually ready they are to deliver God's word to His people. Some of this spiritual dryness is one of the reasons why we have some "dead churches" today.

Preaching is a spiritual act. It is a process of delivering spiritual food to people (spirit beings). It is advisable that that "food" is properly cooked in prayers before delivering it to people. Do not preach what you do not believe. Preach what you live. Let your lifestyle be the message. Preach the undiluted Word of God full of faith, in season and out of season. I am not saying that if you sit under a ministration and you are not blessed that you should blame the preacher. No, if you are indignant or your mind is occupied with earthly cares, the Word of God will not find a home in you. This is why it is demanded of us that when we hear the Word of God, we should harden not our hearts (Hebrews 3:15).

How to Acquire Ginosko?

This knowledge is obtained not by mere intellectual activity, but by the operation of the Holy Spirit subsequent to our acceptance of Christ.

"When the (Holy Spirit) is come, He will convict the world of sin, and of righteousness and of judgment: of sin because they believe not in me, of righteousness because I go to my father and you see me no more; of judgment because the prince of this world is judged"

John 16:8-11

It is the Holy Spirit that gives you the conviction of sin, so you may know God and believe in His righteousness. Now as a believer, He convicts you of righteousness and condemns you not, because there is now no condemnation to them which are in Christ Jesus who walk not after the flesh but after the spirit (Romans 8:1).

He convicts the devil of judgment because the prince of this world has been judged and condemned. Therefore, the Holy Spirit convicts the world of sin and satan of judgment and condemnation, while He makes known to believers their righteousness - John 16:9-11 (Amplified)

"And ye shall know (ginosko) the truth, and the truth shall make you free"

John 8:32

Jesus is the way, truth and the life. The Holy Spirit gives us that conviction to know (ginosko) the truth. Without the truth, there is no way we can be made free. The Holy Spirit's influence on earth touches every sphere; it touches both the believers and the non-believers. With the unbelievers, it reminds them of their sins, that is the guilt of sin and the needs of salvation, and for the believers, it reminds us of our righteousness, the finished work of Christ and our ability, authority to stand in the place of our salvation. Wow! Is that not awesome, to know that the Holy Spirit is there to teach and show you what you need to know about your life and position in Christ?

Finally, we'll conclude this chapter with a quote from a book titled "How to be led by the Holy Spirit" by Peter Tan.

"And ginosko speaks about knowing not only in the spirit man but a knowing that comes to the understanding and the mind. So that was a great degree of Jesus' perception. Jesus had developed himself and His spirit to the extent that when He knew in His spirit, He knew in His understanding perfectly."

Chapter 3

Oida Knowledge

Another kind of knowledge we are going to examine is oida or eido. Oida is the perfect form of the verb eido. Although oida is in perfect tense, it is translated as if it were in the present - "I know". It connotes an idea of "possessed knowledge" rather than the process of "acquiring knowledge." The verb "oida" in the perfect tense means to "know without a doubt, to know for certain, or to acknowledge" depending on the context in which it is used. In the present tense, it expresses the concept of a continued, completed state, meaning "I have come to know (through experience or event)".

Oida is from the same root word as eidon, "to see". It is a perfect tense with a present meaning, signifying primarily "to have seen or perceived."

Inward Consciousness

John Nelson Darby, an Irishman who translated the bible into several languages, wrote of oida as "signifying objective knowledge, what a man has learned or acquired." It may imply "being acquainted with". Oida conveys the thought of what is inward; the inward consciousness in the mind, intuitive knowledge not immediately derived from what is external.

The Difference between Ginosko and Oida Knowledge

We use scriptures to understand scriptures. The best way to understand God's Word is to have a look at other verses. So it is vital we take a look at John 8 in its entirety to see where Jesus used oida and ginosko so as to ascertain what oida really is. After the Pharisee denied the record Jesus bore of Himself, Jesus responded, *"though I bear record of myself, yet my record is true; for I know (eido) whence I came, and whither I go; but you cannot tell whence I come and whither I go"* (John 8:14).

Jesus talks about being aware and conscious of where He came from and His purpose and mission here on earth. Oida conveys the thought of consciousness and awareness. We as Christians need to be aware and conscious of where we are from and where we are going (our purpose on earth). Jesus repeatedly said His Kingdom is not of this world. We are in the world but are not of this world (John 17:14-16).

We came from God and are born of God. Our awareness and consciousness of who we are matters a lot in the race of life. Ignorance of our identity is the avenue for frustration to set in. If you don't know where you came from and where you are going, you will end up going nowhere. Someone once said, "If you don't know where you are going, everywhere will look like the right destination!"

When the Pharisees asked Jesus where his Father was, he responded:

"Ye neither know (eido) me, nor my father; if you had known (eido) me, ye should have known (eido) my father also"

John 8:20

They didn't accept Jesus' identity, so they could not understand the father. They were not aware or conscious of who Jesus was, this is why they couldn't grasp an awareness of the Father. Knowing Jesus, the Word of God, gives you access to the Father.

Jesus warned them that they would die in their sins if they refused to accept Him as the light of the world.

"Then said Jesus unto them, when you have lifted up the son of man, then shall you know (ginosko) that I am He..."

John 8:28

And ye shall know (ginosko) the truth, and the truth will set you free... I know (eido) that you

54

are Abraham's seeds... If you are Abraham's children, you would do the work of Abraham"

John 8:32,37,39(NKJV)

Jesus made them to understand that they would know (ginosko) that He was the Light of the world only after they had crucified Him. They did not believe in Jesus' confirmation of His person and authority when He assured them that if they would keep His Word, they would not die.

"Then said the Jews unto him, now we know (ginosko) that you have a demon. Abraham is dead, and the prophets; and you say, If a man keeps my saying, he shall never taste of death. Yet you have not known him; but I know him: and if I should say, I know him not, I shall be a liar like unto you: but I know him, and keep his saying"

John 8: 52,55

Oida suggests fullness of knowledge while ginosko is an inception or progress in knowledge. This difference can be found in the bible:

a) *"Ye have not known (ginosko) him"* i.e. begun to know but *"I know (oida) Him"* i.e. known him perfectly." John 8:55.

b) "What I do thou knoweth (eido) not; but thou shall know (ginosko) hereafter." Jesus was telling Peter "What I do you perceive not, you do not realize, are not aware of its significance but you'll understand, having that knowledge of it hereafter." John 13:7.

c) "And He said unto them, know ye (eido) not this parable? And how will you know (ginosko) all parables?" Mark 4:13.

Jesus, speaking of natural things on earth, expected them to know (be consciously aware of) these parables, so that they would understand (ginosko) or have that knowledge of spiritual things. The physical realm gives us a glimpse of spiritual things. However, permit me to say that the question was a rhetorical question because Jesus went ahead and gave the answer without waiting for their response. Also, note that it was prophesied that Jesus would speak in parables and some would not understand (Matthew 13:35).

Oida expresses the fact that the object has simply come within the scope of the knower's perception while ginosko implies an active relationship between the one who knows and the person or thing "known".

As Matthew 7:23 ("*I never knew you*") *(ginosko)* suggests, I have never been in an approved connection with you. While *"I know you not (oida)"* suggests you stand in no relation to me.

The "Know Ye Not" Formula

This phrase appears in the New Testament more than 15 times and 10 times in first Corinthians alone. The word used here is "ouk-oidate". Ouk the negation and oidate the second plural of the word *"know ye."* Paul, addressing the believers of the church in

Corinth used this word to emphasize the consciousness of what is in their possession or what they ought to have known; also to explain what had been given to them as well as who they were.

The problem of the church then was not that they had not been provided with certain facts, but rather their lack of awareness or knowledge of what belonged to them. We are going to study some of the verses Paul used; because we are living in the same dispensation; it also relates to us to today. For instance, some Christians have sin problems not because the issue of sin has not been dealt with, but simply because of the lack of oida knowledge. One of the ministerial functions of an evangelist is to exalt, which implies to help us elevate that which is already there. So when an evangelist ministers or a message is preached, you find yourself spiritually lifted, you become aware or conscious of your position or status in Christ. As believers, our position in Christ remains unchanged, but our awareness or consciousness of this position can vary.

Sudden deeper awareness can come as a result of the ministration of an Evangelist. Exaltation is simply an awakening or consciousness of that which is already there.

Christ did everything and He said *"it is finished"* (John 19:30). When He said this, He meant just what he said: it is finished; your problems, sickness, pain and grief are finished. He did not mean that it is partially finished and He will come and rescue us from some. No! It is finished means it is finished. The question is; why then do the problems seem to abide or reoccur, when it has been dealt with on the cross already? Why sin again when the price has been paid?

Do you know the problem? Lack of this kind of knowledge is the problem. This is why Jesus and Paul preached to the people asking: *"Know ye not..."* Don't you know that you have been bought with a price; don't you know that he that is joined to a harlot is one flesh with that harlot?

"Know ye not, that to whom ye yield yourselves servants to obey, his servants ye are to whom ye obey; whether of sin unto death, or of obedience unto righteousness?"

Romans 6:16

Don't you know that you are a slave to whatever you yield to? So I urge you to submit yourself to the Holy Spirit. Don't yield to anger; for anger is the short road to danger. Therefore don't be a slave to anger. Don't yield to the voice of revenge, revenge belongs to God and not to you. God will repay, so please don't fight back.

Even though multitudes have received Christ, you can still find some people yielding to the wrong voices. No doubt you might wonder at times why you still get the same negative results even though you are a Christian. This however depends on whom you yield to, because you are a slave to whomsoever you yield to. No mercy! This is a law. Don't blame God for any naughtiness caused by you. He has already given us the wisdom to yield to the right Spirit. This was the problem of the early church and is also a problem in the practice of today's Christianity. People yield to the wrong voice and as such become slaves to a wrong spirit. I pray that you shall not be one of them. May you find grace and boldness to say no to every slavish control by a wrong spirit over your life in Jesus' name.

"Know ye not, brethren, (for I speak to them that know the law,) how that the law hath dominion over a man as long as he liveth?"

Romans 7:1

Obviously if you don't have oida knowledge of what has been dealt with on the cross, you will suffer in bondage. Look at this simple example: many years ago when I surrendered my life to Jesus Christ, I threw away all the jeans pants I had. Most preachers around me at that time were preaching against wearing jeans and you could hardly find anyone wearing them to church. It was regarded as unbelievers' attire and as a true Christian you were forbidden to wear them.   Therefore, I decided to throw mine away as I didn't want to be unequally yoked with unbelievers as was being proclaimed. I had lots of *do not's* in my head. Wearing jeans was a problem because I believed that it was for the unbelievers! Imagine how devastating that was! Thank God His mercy covered me during that period of time and I didn't quit the faith; after all my heart was right and seeking to please God more than focusing on any outward appearance. Later, I got the oida knowledge of what had already been dealt with on the cross and what the law is all about. Now I live a spiritual life full of the Spirit. I walk in the Spirit and it is only by the Spirit that I know what to do and what not to do. Don't let a particular law entangle you, walk by the law of the Spirit and the law of love and you will be free from bondage. I have observed how laws have trapped many and tied them in bondage, taking them off the straight road of Christianity. Then you will later hear such people saying that they are tired of Christianity and can't keep the laws and that it is difficult. You know, most of the people who have left the Christian faith for something else were entangled by the bondage through misappropriation of the law. They struggled to live by their own efforts and then finally they succumbed, realizing it was impossible. No options left other than to withdraw! However, this book is not about the law, but you can carry out further research to see that misunderstanding of the law has entangled many lives in bondage. *Know ye not* that we have been set free from these? When you have that oida knowledge, that I have been set free from the law of sin and death (Romans 7:6). When you get this consciousness, you will live a stress free Christian life in righteousness.

"Know ye not that ye are the temple of God, and that the Spirit of God dwelleth in you?"

1 Corinthians 3:16

As I mentioned earlier, the issue is not that your body is not the temple of the Holy Spirit. It is the temple of the Holy Spirit. It is not just mental knowledge though, it requires a deeper knowledge to access and comprehend this divine truth. The devil or you yourself may mess with your body when you don't have this comprehensive knowledge of the truth. When you know (oida), that your body is the temple of the Holy Spirit, you won't joke with it. You will laugh at the devil when he tries to throw sickness on that body. Your body has been bought with a price. The devil or sickness cannot try to loiter around someone else's property. You can only seize the property of a powerless man, not a strong one.

"Know ye not that your bodies are the members of Christ? Shall I then take the members of Christ, and make them the members of an harlot? God forbid. What? know ye not that he which is joined to an harlot is one body? For two, saith he, shall be one flesh. What? Know ye not that your body is the temple of the Holy Ghost which is in you, which ye have of God, and ye are not your own?"

1 Corinthians 6:15-16, 19

Your body is a super giant property, vehemently owned by a divine supreme authority - God. Whichever devil wants to deal with your voice, talent, health, gifts, etc. cannot be compared with the owner of this property. Therefore he cannot succeed! Stand up in faith, become consciously aware of these facts, resist the devil and he will flee away.

The Supreme Being who owns your life says you have been given authority to trample over serpents and scorpions. You have been given an opportunity to speak over situations and they must respond accordingly. Your words are commands. He has given you the words and wisdom to override any situation. Your adversary cannot gainsay nor resist this authority. Speak man, over that problem and for sure it will disappear.

You have been given authority to proclaim judgment and even to judge angels.

"Know ye not that we shall judge angels? How much more things that pertain to this life?"

1 Corinthians 6:3

"Examine yourselves, whether ye be in the faith; prove your own selves. Know ye not your own selves, how that Jesus Christ is in you, except ye be reprobates? But I trust that ye shall know that we are not reprobates"

2 Corinthians 13:5,6

Jesus Christ is in you! There is only one thing that desecrates that power in you and that is sin or the cares of the world. When you hook or cleave to the world you become worldly. You become materialistic and controlled by perishable things. It becomes very easy for the devil to tie a rope around your neck and pull you down to perpetual emptiness. No matter how small it may be, never give in to the things of this world. Don't let him lure you into it.

"Your glorying is not good. Know ye not that a little leaven leaveneth the whole lump?"

1 Corinthians 5:6

"Know ye not that the unrighteous shall not inherit the Kingdom of God? Be not deceived: neither fornicators, nor idolaters, nor

adulterers, nor effeminate, nor abusers of themselves with mankind"

1 Corinthians 6:9

"...know ye not that the friendship of the world is enmity with God? Whosoever therefore will be a friend of the world is the enemy of God."

James 4:4

Therefore, my friend, don't be an enemy of God. It may sound light but you don't know how dangerous that can be. We are passers-by in this world. You came here for a mission, I urge you to finish well. Life is a race but remember you are not running alone; there are a multitude of others running with you but at their own pace. You might be in India, France, Switzerland, USA, Ghana etc; but I encourage you to run well.

"Know ye not that they which run in a race run all, but one receiveth the prize? So run, that ye may obtain"

1 Corinthians 9:24

Run so fast that you will receive the prize. Run like a good soldier of Christ. Do not listen to the philosophical reasoning as to why God allegedly does not exist or why you only have to live and die then nothing else. Life is beyond just living. There is more to life than you could ever imagine. God has given to the human race supernatural powers to unlock and lock every situation in life. Your consciousness gives you access to deeper life treasures and oida knowledge is a type of conscious knowledge. A man with no hope or future is a man who has lost consciousness and awareness of his personality. You can't be who you don't know you are. You only become who you know you are. This is the work most motivational speakers are trying to make us realize. Self realization is the beginning of self fulfillment. A blind man cannot lead himself. Only a person who sees and knows where he is going can navigate himself. You are not blind! Be conscious, especially in the area of God consciousness, Spirit consciousness. Only then will you be able to steer your life and thus give it meaning.

Note that there are several things that have been granted to you. It only takes the oida knowledge to have it in your possession. There is power in being conscious of what you have or who you are. I pray that you will know (oida) what has been freely given to you and at the end, like Christ, be able to say *"I know who I am"*."*I am a king, I am a chosen generation..."*

Chapter 4

Epiginosko Knowledge

We have understood from the previous chapter that oida knowledge is that absolute knowledge that gives us the consciousness or awareness of what has been freely given to us by Christ. Also that oida knowledge helps us to tap the treasure that lies within us. It gives us access to our own possessions and the consciousness of it makes us gain from it.

This knowledge (Epiginosko) is a compound word. Epi – meaning upon or further, and ginosko is what we have already explained in Chapter 2. Before going further, I want you to understand that Epiginosko is different from Epignosis (which we will look at later).

Epiginosko is a verb, while Epignosis is a noun. Epiginosko is the process or the road leading to Epignosis, while Epignosis is the result that is visible. You can't see belief, but you can see faith. It is thy faith that makes you whole and faith is the result of your belief.

Inside faith, there is belief and there can't be faith without belief. Belief is not the end result, it is simply the process. It is the means to an end. It is what you need in order to be healed. It is taking action. It is a continuous act that ends when it comes in contact with faith. When this happens, the result becomes visible. New Testament believers don't have problems with faith; they have problems with their belief. We live by the faith of Christ Jesus and the seed of Faith has been planted in us. As a result, we have a measure of faith (Galatians 2:20 and Romans 12:3). It is therefore our belief system that quickens us to faith and leads us to the state of rest.

Epiginosko in the same way is the catalyst for Epignosis. It is the undeniable process that cannot be avoided. When you speak of Epiginosko, you speak of action. It puts action in place and thus drives you to a state of rest. Ginosko establishes the relationship with Christ. Even though you've received Christ, you can still miss this relationship. This is because you can have ginosko and still be carnally minded. You can still be a sinner even when you have received the ginosko knowledge of God.

"Because that, when they knew God, they glorified [him] not as God, neither were thankful; but became vain in their imaginations, and their foolish heart was darkened. And even as they did not like to retain God in [their] knowledge, God gave them over to a reprobate mind, to do those things which are not convenient"

Romans 1:21,28

Therefore, ginosko is not enough. God wants you to not only know Him (Ginosko) but to fully participate in knowing Him (Epiginosko) in order to attain exact knowledge, or to become what you know (Epignosis).

What is Epiginosko?

It is the advanced knowledge of ginosko. It sometimes implies a special participation in the object known and it is gives greater weight to what is stated. It emphasizes one's participation in what is known. It is this knowledge that unites the subject and the object. It unites the knower and the thing known.

As mentioned above, the instance in the book of Romans 1:32, where they had ginosko; it is stated that they knew God through epiginosko knowledge. It states that *they knew the judgment of God, that they which committed such things which they committed are worthy of death, even those who take pleasure in it.* Here epiginosko (knowing the judgment of God) suggests knowing full well and in Romans 1:21, ginosko (they knew God) suggests that they could not avoid the perception.

"And ye shall know the truth, and the truth shall make you free...."

John 8:32

"Forbidding to marry, and commanding to abstain from meats, which God hath created to be received with thanksgiving of them which believe and know the truth"

1 Timothy 4:3

In the above mentioned verses, knowing the truth is emphasized. 1 Timothy 4:3, *"them which believe and know the truth"* talks about you participating in knowing the truth while John 8:32 talks about knowing the truth and the truth thus setting you free.

You did nothing to know the truth. You just know the truth; it is revelation knowledge from God. Ginosko establishes your relationship while epiginosko goes further to unite your relationship with Him. It unites the subject with the object, i.e. you and the truth. 1 Timothy 4:3 speaks of knowing the truth already and continuing in relationship, having

74

rules and laws while in John 8:32, Jesus was talking to people who had not even taken the first step (ginosko). So He was talking about them knowing Him (the Truth), and He 'shall' set them free. After having been set free, there is need of knowing (epiginosko) or having knowledge of the truth.

If we observe where the scripture talks about knowing the grace of God, in some instances it uses epiginosko while in others, ginosko.

"Since we heard of your faith in Christ Jesus, and of the love [which ye have] to all the saints, For the hope which is laid up for you in heaven, whereof ye heard before in the word of the truth of the gospel; Which is come unto you, as [it is] in all the world; and bringeth forth fruit, as [it doth] also in you, since the day ye heard [of it], and KNEW THE GRACE OF GOD IN TRUTH"

Colossians 1:4-6

Here, Paul is writing to the saints who have known the grace of God and are continuing in the grace of God. The word epiginosko is used to describe them knowing the grace of God in truth. Notice that it involves not just knowing the grace, but acting. Their actions and love for God were visible. People heard of their faith which started from the day they knew (epiginosko) God. It is a knowledge you relate with and continue in. It has nothing to do with stagnation. Paul didn't say we heard of your faith that has ceased or we have heard of your faith that no longer bears fruits; rather he explained that it bringeth forth fruits in them since the day they knew that grace. Hallelujah! Epiginosko is not a one-time knowledge. It is the knowledge that you relate with and continue in. It puts actions in place.

Let us study the scriptures that talk about knowing the grace of God without using the word "ginosko".

"For YE KNOW THE GRACE OF OUR LORD JESUS Christ, that, though he was rich, yet for your sakes he became poor, that ye through his poverty might be rich"

2 Corinthians 8:9

Here, emphasis is placed on knowing the grace of God *"ginoskoly"*. You just know without you relating to it. Paul refers to the grace of God that has come to the gentile believers and by this grace; JESUS became poor for our sake so that through His poverty, we the gentile believers might become rich. In this case, you have complete knowledge of what has been done and packaged for you. It takes your participation in the grace (epiginosko) for you to benefit from it.

Did you notice it says that He (Jesus) did something so that you might become something as well? He became poor not that riches should come to you automatically, but that "you might become rich." You might or you might not. If it was automatic, it will come to you without your consent, meaning every believer would become rich even without knowledge. However, it is not automatic, it takes your involvement. You can still be poor and still go to Heaven. It's your choice. You can choose to relate to what you know (ginosko) then that's epiginosko because you have applied further participation to what you know. So when you relate with that which you know, you will have the result and your faith will be heard of.

Though He became poor so that we might become rich, the question then remains, why are some Christians still dwelling in poverty? This is because He became poor so that we should become rich, but not automatically. Lack of knowledge is the principal cause of all unsolved problems. Riches come through our involvement and use of the truth we know. Ginosko is a full package of what God has done and delivered to us. It takes our participation in this knowledge for us to enjoy it fullness and only then shall we become aware of that package (oida). So what are we supposed to do in order to unleash this package? A lot of scriptures tell us what to do. If you study further in 2 Corinthians 8, Paul emphasizes this 'doing' aspect. *"Now therefore perform the **doing of it**; that as there was a readiness to will, so there may **be a performance*** *also out of that which you have."*(2 Corinthians 8:11).

It is the lack of this doing part that accounts for the bulk of sleeping Christians that we have nowadays. A lot of people are sitting and sleeping, while expecting automatic riches. God is not a jackpot player or a magician. Wake up man! Wake up as a good soldier of Christ and work. Jesus said that His father works so we too must work. Here I'm not talking about taking numerous hours of overtime a day at your job that is slavery! I'm talking about productive work that is working on your visions and life purposes.

We must be doers, not hearers only. Faith involves action, not words and mere dreams. If it was automatic (ginosko) without your participation in it (epiginosko), then every Christian would be a billionaire by now. Today, some are and some are not because wealth creation requires you to act upon specific knowledge.

How to Obtain Epiginosko

"You will know (epiginosko) them by their fruits. Do men gather grapes from thorn bushes or figs from thistles? Therefore by their fruits you will know (epignosis) them"

Matthew 7:16,20

As I mentioned earlier, epiginosko has to do with the process, the action, or the doing aspect of our life. It is an advanced knowledge of ginosko. We possess this *knowing* by seeing the action. You will see the fruits and you will *know*. The type of fruits you produce can enable you to have epiginosko knowledge. This determines the actions we take.

"And when he came out, he could not speak unto them: and they perceived that he had seen a vision in the temple: for he beckoned unto them, and remained speechless"

Luke 1:22

Zacharias came out of the temple and was unable to speak. The congregation looked at

80

him (his muteness) and they immediately perceived (epiginosko) that he had seen a vision. What you see must not only be physical or tangible things. You can perceive thoughts and imaginations and you can know the outcome (Luke 5:22). Note that epiginosko also means to see, to perceive, to sense, etc. So you can see (epiginosko) the acts, you can perceive (epiginosko) the thoughts, you can sense (epiginosko) the spirit and you'll know the result.

Examples:

Let us study some more scripture verses

1. When a woman who was a sinner knew (epiginosko) that Jesus was around, she brought an expensive perfume. *"And, behold, a woman in the city, which was a sinner, when she knew that Jesus sat at meat in the Pharisee's house, brought an alabaster box of ointment"*. Luke 7:37

2. When power left Jesus, He immediately perceived or sensed what had happened. He asked, *"Who touched my garment?"*. The woman who tapped His power was instantly healed.

Her action was in the spiritual realm. She drew this power spiritually through her belief. Jesus immediately perceived (epiginosko) this, because of what was going on in the spiritual realm, while the others were dumbfounded.

"And Jesus, immediately knowing in himself that virtue had gone out of him, turned him about in the press, and said, who touched my clothes?"

Mark 5:30

3. Your thoughts are not just empty fantasies. They are actions that are taking place in the invisible realm. You become what you think! In other words, you cause to be in place everything that you allow your thoughts to dwell upon. So be careful what you think about.

In Mark 2, when the scribes were sitting and began to reason in their hearts that Jesus was speaking blasphemy since He claimed He had the power to forgive sins.

"And immediately when Jesus perceived in his spirit that they so reasoned within themselves,

he said unto them, why reason ye these things in your hearts?"

Mark 2:8

Jesus immediately perceived (epiginosko) as a result of their invisible act (reasoning).

4. In Acts 4, when the crowd saw the boldness of Peter, they immediately perceived or knew that he had been with Jesus (Acts 4:13).

5. In Acts 4 again, when Peter was released from prison by an angel, he went to the house of Mary the mother of John, where many were gathered praying. He stood at the gate and knocked the door of the gate. When the young lady who went to open the door "heard" his voice, she immediately knew (epiginosko) that it was Peter. She was so excited that she could not open the door because of what she had just "known". This knowledge puts action in place, so you can see the act and know the result. You become possessed with knowledge as a result of an act which may be visible or invisible.

One last example for clarification purposes can be found in Mathew 14:35: "*And when the men of that place had knowledge (epiginosko) of him, they sent out into all that country and brought all that were diseased*". When the population knew of Jesus i.e. had epiginosko knowledge of Jesus, they acted by bringing sick people to him. They knew who He was; this is why they could bring together the sick and the bedridden, that they might come into contact with Jesus. This knowledge lays emphasis on your participation in what is known. It perfectly unites the subject and the object to discover, to ascertain or to determine.

Ginosko Plus Epiginosko Produces Epignosis

"Whether there be knowledge (gnosis), it shall vanish away. For we know (ginosko) in part and we prophesy in part"

1 Corinthians 13:8,9

84

Knowledge that is scientific in nature shall vanish away. We have that revelation knowledge in part, so we speak forth by divine inspiration in part; however, if we know in full then we will utter or declare things which can only be by divine inspiration, in full. (I hope you already have an idea of what the above verse is talking about. That we know in part does not necessarily mean that we cannot come to full knowledge).

"But when that which is perfect is come, then that which is in part shall be done away. For now we see through a glass, darkly; but then face to face. Now I know in part; then shall I know (epiginosko) even as also I am known (epiginosko)"

1 Corinthians 13:10,12

From this passage we can understand that the writer through the inspiration of the Holy Spirit is talking about growth in knowledge. This is why in verse 11, it says "when *I was a child, I spoke as a child, I understood as a child, I thought as a child. But when I became a man, I put away childish things*". Childhood is not in size, it is in knowledge. The difference between a child and a man here is in knowledge, not in birth dates, height, size or shape. So the scripture says that we have ginosko in part, but when that perfect knowledge (epignosis) shall come, it is going to replace the ginosko knowledge. Amen! Remember, the Greek word *"Epi"* means upon, further or advance. Epiginosko is the process and epignosis is the end. Ginosko is not going to vanish. It's going to be advanced, but gnosis (scientific) knowledge shall vanish. We can't experience God in the intellectual realm but we know Him in the spirit. The soul of man is limited from experiencing the fullness of God's knowledge.

In this life when you grow, let's say from childhood to adulthood, your childhood vanishes gradually and not instantly on one Saturday morning. What happens is that as you grow in knowledge, the lesser knowledge becomes replaced by greater knowledge. You become replaced by a greater man with a greater knowledge. The scripture below further explains something very interesting and vital, *"Now I know (ginosko) in part but then shall I know (epiginosko) even as also I am known (epiginosko)"*. "You shall know as you are known" refers to epignosis. So as you grow deeper, you become what you know that is the exact or precise and correct knowledge of what is known (epiginosko). It is with this knowledge that you become the substance of what you know. It is the undeniable and the inseparable union with the object known. You shall know as you are known which is equal to epignosis.

Therefore we conclude this chapter by saying that ginosko is what you know without any participation. It is the complete package you receive. Epiginosko is the continuity in the exploration of that package. Oida is awareness and consciousness of it when explored. Gnosis is your intellectual (soulish) participation of it and finally, epignosis is the end result. We shall talk more about this in Chapter 8. So, beloved in the Lord, I urge you to bear fruit after having understood what epiginosko is. It is the fruit bearing process of your Christian walk. Do it with love and peace, and you shall receive a greater reward and greater grace shall be imparted upon you. May you continue in grace always!

Chapter 5

Proginosko Knowledge

"Why are you disturbing me, man of God? God already knows that I am going to be a prostitute, one of my brothers a burglar and the other, a pastor. We have been predestinated to be where we are today. So when the time comes for me to be born again, I will be. If it is God's will for me to be born again, I'm going to be born-again. God knows everything about my life, everything has been planned and some people are destined to go to Hell and others to Heaven. We cannot change it!"

What a dilemma! This is a peculiar problem in our religious world today. This was the type of conversation I had with a lady while evangelizing to her. We sometimes believe that God has predestinated our life and our choices so free will does not matter. This is the dilemma that has taken over the faith and the lives of many. We believe things have been predetermined to produce the results we see today. Yes, things have been programmed ahead of time. God works with a system. He formed the world systematically in such a way that everything works in its order. Things reproduce after their kind and multiplication takes place without His direct intervention.

God has foreknowledge of creation's outcomes and that is why He created them. He is an architect: He designed and structured the world in the way that He wants it to function. He knows the result of every action. He had the picture of how creation would be even before the beginning of the world. After He created everything in the world, He then formed man and gave man the authority to handle those things which He created. He gave man the authority to have dominion and rule over what He had created. Then He later declared to man:

"Be fruitful and multiply and replenish the earth, and subdue it: and have dominion over

*the fish of the sea and over every living thing
that moveth upon the earth"*

Genesis 1:28

This was His declaration, which wasn't a
choice. It was a command that man would be
what He said man would be. Man will be
fruitful, multiply, replenish the earth and have
dominion. This is how He has created man to
be. He knows what He wants man to be and to
become. He has a goal and a purpose for man
and that is why He embarked upon the
creation journey.

God declares that He knew us even before we
were born. He created us to be conformed to
the image of His beloved Son.

*"For whom He did foreknow (proginosko), He
also did predestinate to be conformed to the
image of his son, that he might be the first born
among many brethren"*

Romans 8:29

He clearly said from the beginning, *"Let us
make man in our image, after our likeness".*

91

(Genesis 1:26). Man is made after His likeness and image. Man is created like God, and with His image.

The main thing we wish to study here is the word "proginosko", translated as "foreknow". We are going to study what it refers to and what He knows us to be and made us for. He said to Jeremiah:

"Before I formed thee in the belly I knew thee; and before thou camest forth out of the womb I sanctified thee; and I ordained thee a prophet unto the nations"

Jeremiah 1:10

This means God had a foreknowledge of Jeremiah. The word "foreknow" is the same as "proginosko". Proginosko is a compound word, *pro* (before) and *ginosko* (knowledge). It is the pre-knowing of things or persons. It also means to foreordain, know, or know beforehand. It only occurs five times in the New Testament but its impact on the Christian philosophical reasoning is tremendous. We are going to study some of the verses to understand its full context and meaning. In the introduction to this chapter, we see a lady complaining that she need not do anything because her actions have already been preordained. So she's simply just living out what God has planned in advance. Her opinion therefore is that God has preordained even the thoughts of her mind and heart. Does that really mean God knows the things we are going to do tomorrow? And the thoughts we are going to think on? This is like questioning the omniscience of God-*THE ALL KNOWING, right?* We say God is omniscient: true! This means He knows every detail of our lives. However, there is a misunderstanding somewhere. Let's see what omniscient means. It means the ability to know everything that there is to know. It is to know everything about a character, including past history, thoughts, and feelings. It is from the Latin word *omnis* meaning all and *sciens* meaning knowing. Obviously, God is the all knowing God and perfect in knowledge (Job 37:16). He knows the past, the present and the future. Because of this omniscient power of God, does it mean that our actions tomorrow and thoughts have been programmed ahead of time without our choice?

Let's see some of the scriptures in which proginosko (foreknow) was used.

"I say then, has God cast away His people? Certainly not! For I also am an Israelite, of the seed of Abraham, of the tribe of Benjamin. God has not cast away His people whom He foreknew. Or do you not know what the scripture says of Elijah, how he pleads with God against Israel, saying"

Romans 11:1-2

In verse 2, the word *foreknow* is the word proginosko. Here, it simply means God has not rejected his people whom He knew before, not predetermined. This is historical knowing or knowing in times past, not knowing as predestination. As in Acts 26:5 *"Which **knew** (proginosko) me from the beginning, if they will testify, that after the most straight sect of our religion I lived a Pharisee"*. Paul testifying before King Agrippa that most of the Jews knew him

94

before or had proginosko knowledge of him as a Pharisee. Now, look at proginosko in the case of Jesus, preordained by God:

"He indeed was foreordained (proginosko) before the foundation of the world, but was manifest in these last times for you who through Him believe in God, who raised Him from the dead and gave Him glory, so that your faith and hope are in God"

1 Peter 1:20-21

God foreordained Jesus and Jeremiah for the work which He called them to do. It implies God has foreordained us to walk in His perfect will for us. There is a perfect way that God has ordained for every one of us.

Will Power

When God created man, He gave man the will power to make his own choices. He gave man this will power so that he could produce whatever results he wants to achieve. Whatever choices that man makes determine

95

the outcome. Though God has given man this sole authority to make his choices, He has the perfect plan of what He wants man to become. He wants man to be conformed to the image of His dear beloved Son. He wants man to be like Him. This is what He preordained him for; but this is a choice. It is man's choice to decide if he will walk in that preordained path or not.

God is all knowing, He knows man's thoughts. He actually doesn't know your futuristic thoughts or actions because they don't exist. The complete results of the future are not planned as in the detailed sense of it. Genesis 6:6 says *"And it repented the Lord that He had made man on Earth, and it grieved him to his heart."* He was shocked to see man's results. This was not the main reason for His creation of man. He didn't plan for man to succumb to sin. The wickedness of man was great upon the earth and the Lord regretted that He had made him. Will you tell me the Lord preordained this? No, He didn't, neither did He know this event aforetime. He had no proginosko knowledge of this event.

I know sometimes we try humanly to make God look like just a good guy. We defend Him in every good thing. Just like a thief will steal and say God saved him and He wasn't caught. That wasn't God because He didn't send him in the first place! We try to give Him the credit in our human way without knowing that rather we are endangering His personality and thus putting the world in fatal confusion. We can't make him look nicer with our human understanding than what He says. Take His Word the way He says it and He will give you the full inspiration of it. For example, if you don't train a child in the way that he should go, then he will likewise become something else. Your will, decision and the training you offer can make a difference in the life of the child. God knows that if you train the child, he become a better person and if you don't, he might become a riffraff for example. It all depends on you. You have the delegated authority to prune his character, attitude and personality. Just like Job, God had absolute confidence that he wouldn't deny him no matter what Satan would do to him. He told

Satan, go and try him and you will see that he is different. His personality and will were grounded in the love of God. There was no instability in him.

The outcome and results of life depend on us because we have been given absolute will power and delegated authority.

The will power that God gave man has the power to make man whatever he decides to be. It has the ability to determine what happens in his life. Even the devil cannot subjugate this power. It is solely in the power of man to determine his own outcome. He has the power to determine whom he yields his will to, whom he obeys and whom he disobeys; however, when you yield this will power to God's control, He leads you to His purpose for your life. He cannot force you to yield or surrender this power to Him. He simply presents His request to you and you respond accordingly. What does surrendering your life to Christ mean? It means giving Him your will so He can take you to His pre-planned life for you.

Thoughts Are Occurrences

Decisions not yet made do not exist; so God doesn't know such things, but whatever is in the realm of the mind is known by Him because it has already occurred. It exists. Your present thoughts are an occurrence. Even if they don't produce anything now, their outcomes are already known by God. Thoughts are more real than what you see. Permit me to say that thoughts are events that are pending. The reality of what we see in the physical realm has already taken place in the spiritual realm. Not already pre-planned but already occurred and its existence later becomes visible in the physical realm. Let us look at some examples. When the devil entered the mind of Judas Iscariot, the future event became clearly known. Jesus unveiled to the disciples that one of them would betray him. He said, *"the one who has dipped his hand into the bowl with me will betray me"* Matthew 26:23 (NIV). This event had already occurred in the invisible realm! In the physical, it was simply pending in the realm of thoughts. The real world is not what we see with our visible eyes. The invisible world is more real than this visible world. We are only reproducing events in this visible world which have already taken place in the invisible world. Whatever you communicate in your thought can be read and its effects can be seen. Your thoughts are the reasons for your daily actions. This is why we are forewarned to guard our thoughts and to think about those things that are lovely, of good report, things that are praiseworthy, are pure, and are noble (Philippians 4:8).

Another example we should look at is the instance in which Jesus said *that "whosoever looks on a woman to lust after her has committed adultery with her already in his heart."* Matthew 5:28. At that moment adultery has already been committed. The important part isn't the physical aspect but the invisible aspect because when it is in the thoughts or heart, It has already occurred so all that remains is the physical manifestation. It is difficult to have intercourse without having had the thought of it in your mind! Until something occurs in the invisible realm of life, it won't occur in the visible world.

For you to commit fornication or adultery, Satan will first initiate that in your thought. He will then make sure he follows you up with that thought by building blocks of it until it manifests itself in the physical. Then when it occurs, he will say mission accomplished!

Until your heart, your thoughts, your mind acts in the invisible, nothing will be manifested in the physical world. Permit me again to say that Abraham had already sacrificed Isaac before he was divinely stopped by God. God had to shout saying *"Now I know..."* (Genesis 22:12). *"Now I know..."* It sounds like He didn't know before, right? This was because only when the action had already occurred in the invisible realm could God afterward intervene in the physical. You're a product of your thought and you become what you think!

Now talking about proginosko-foreknowing, if you read the scripture plainly as it is written you will realize that God spoke some things as if He wasn't really aware of the future. Statements such as "perhaps *they will listen, so that they'll repent"*, *"so they may know that I am the Lord"*, etc.

"Perhaps everyone will listen and turn from his evil way, that I may relent concerning the calamity which I purpose to bring on them because of the evil of their doings"

Jeremiah 26:3

Statements such as "for *if you thoroughly amend your ways and doings..."* (Jeremiah 7:5-7), shows us that the result hasn't occurred yet and God doesn't know, therefore has not predestinated the outcome of that event. Don't try to play God as a *"nice guy"* by trying to defend the context. Trying to change it meaning will simply bring in confusion and destroy the relationship through which God wants man to understand Him. God created man in His likeness and He wants man to understand Him in his human capacity using divine knowledge. By looking at God, man is being transformed into the image of God. Remember if such an event already has a thought placement, then it has occurred. A thought placement is a vision or dream that empowers it occurrences. A life without vision is a life moving in haphazard puzzles that is a matter of chance and luck.

Obviously, God knows *everything* (*every-thing*) and thoughts are things. Whatever is not a thing does not exist. As long as it can't be found in the invisible and visible realm, it doesn't exist!

Life is a journey and there is an end result to every journey. There is a prize in every race. We are in the race of life and God wants us to be winners. He has predestinated us to be winners, not failures. This is a global plan which every individual can decide to divert from or follow. Those who are in Hell weren't predestined to be in Hell. They made their choice to be there. Some who died untimely deaths weren't programmed to die as such, their actions predetermined this outcome.

Perhaps you may not agree with me that those who are in Hell have not been programmed by God to go there. There are people who assume that God has purposed for some people to be in Hell and others in Heaven. Well, that is the same as saying He has prepared some to be infected with HIV or die through an accident etc. These can't be true, for sickness is against His will and whatever is against His will is also against His plans and His purpose for man.

I strongly believe God has a universal plan for mankind and an individual plan for each person depending on their relationship with Him. Deuteronomy 29:29 tells us that the plans He has revealed belong to us and our children forever and the secret things belong to Him. You may not have the answer to every detailed question regarding His pre-planned purpose for your life, but as you study, fellowship and enquire from Him more, He will make known His plans for you and your children.

"Who gave Himself for our sins so that He might rescue us from this present evil age, according to the will of our God and Father, to whom be the glory forevermore. Amen. I am amazed that you are so quickly deserting Him who called you by the grace of Christ, for a

different gospel. But even if we, or an angel from heaven, should preach to you a gospel contrary to what we have preached to you, he is to be accursed! As we have said before, so I say again now, if any man is preaching to you a gospel contrary to what you received, he is to be accursed!"

Galatians 1:4,5,6,8-9 (NASB)

Generally, God doesn't want anybody to perish and it is not His will or desire that any should perish. He wants all to come to repentance and to walk according to His purpose. When you accept Christ into your life, you begin a journey into the predestined plans God originally set for you. It is a transition from the kingdom of darkness into the kingdom of light (Colossians 1:13). It is a transition from the kingdom of an unknown purpose to the kingdom of a known purpose. This doesn't mean all of your decisions will be planned or have been planned by Him. It will depend on how you yield to Him.

As a born again child of God, He orders your steps. He takes charge of your life and leads you to walk according to His will. It is a spiritual walk. It is that kind of walk in which you now walk in the spirit and you walk as the child of Light (Ephesians 5:8). His light enlightens your steps and you begin to know who you are and where you are going. Hallelujah! His word becomes a lamp to your feet and a light to your path. Here you have overcome the deeds of the world which war against the spirit that is leading your life.

Understanding Your Divine Purpose

How can you know the purpose for which God created and predestined your life? Why were you created and why do you live? Is there a reason for your life? Is there a reason why God took His time and made you a personality? Perhaps He just wanted you to till the land like and live without purpose? No, there is a plan and a purpose for you to fulfill. No architect will draw a plan that has no purpose. No manufacturer will build anything that has no function. Only a mad man can build something without a reason for it and God is not a mad man. Therefore, for you to know your purpose you have to enquire from God.

Regarding purpose, Dr. Myles Monroe said the following: "Purpose is the original intent in the mind of the Creator that motivated Him to create a particular item. It is the why that explains the reason for existence". Every product is a product of purpose. Therefore for you to know the purpose of something you have to go to the creator of the thing. You simply discover it because it has been there before you were even created. My senior pastor and mentor Sunday Adelaja normally says that one of the ways to discover your purpose is to know where your love and pain meet or intercept. When you are wholly or passionately consumed by its fulfillment or the way it can be done, then that can be an indication that you have been called into that sphere. (Of course that's not all you need to know, for there are many more factors to be considered). Dr. Mike Murdock also said: "Your passion is a pointer to the problem you were created to solve".

Since God is the giver of purpose, for you to know the purpose of your life you have to know His Word. He reveals himself through His Word. His Word is the foundation and the light to every true purpose. His Word will help you discern what is good and what is evil. You might be going down the wrong path but His Word will help you find your way out.

"For the word of God is quick and powerful... and is a discerner of the thoughts and intents of the heart"

Hebrews 4:12

His Word is Spirit and God is Spirit. Therefore, when His Word lives in you, His Spirit will also live in you. And God will reveal the purpose of your life through His Spirit that lives in you.

"For who knows a person's thoughts except their own spirit within them? In the same way

no one knows the thoughts of God except the Spirit of God"

1 Corinthians 2:11 NIV

"I the LORD search the heart and examine the mind, to reward each person according to their conduct, according to what their deeds deserve"

Jeremiah 17:10 NIV

However, a God-given purpose will always be God and people centered, never self centered. God never gives egoistic purposes: such purposes originate from the devil. A God-given purpose will always relate to the uplifting of society.

Finally, in conclusion of this topic, I would like to point out that God has a general plan and purpose for every individual, and for mankind as a whole. For you to walk in this plan; you have to *YIELD* your will to Him. Allowing Him to be the Lord of your life gives Him absolute control over you. It gives Him the ability to come to you through His Spirit and lead your life. He is the vine and you are the branches.

God therefore has predestined us to be conformed to the image of his son Jesus Christ (Romans 8:29). This is why He has made His grace available to all, *"For the grace of God that bringeth salvation has appeared to all men"* (Titus 2:1). This grace gives us an open invitation to be among the elects of God; but this invitation can only be accepted by our own will and desire; which enables us to align ourselves with His plan and purpose in our lives. God has been patiently waiting for you to align your will to His predestined life for you.

"The Lord is not slow about His promise, as some count slowness, but is patient toward you, not wishing for any to perish but for all to come to repentance"

2 Peter 3:9

"This is good and acceptable in the sight of God our Savior, who desires all men to be

110

saved and to come to the knowledge of the truth"

1 Timothy 2:3-4

God desires all men to be saved: to be conformed to the image of His beloved Son. He desires all men to walk in His righteousness and holiness. He wants all men to be born of Him. This is a global invitation that takes personal faith for it to be actualized in your life. It is therefore a freewill choice that *"whosoever believes in him shall be saved",* not that some have been programmed to be saved and others have not. He wants all to be saved! I urge you therefore to surrender your life totally to His control and let Him make known His proginosko plan and purpose for your life. It only requires a simple prayer of acknowledgement. Acknowledge the work He has done on the cross for you and accept Him into your life without delay. He has been standing at the door of your heart knocking. Invite him in and He will come and be your Lord for forever and ever!

111

Chapter 6

Gnostos Knowledge

Gnostos means known or notable. It appears fifteen times in the Bible, 10 of which are in the book of Acts alone. It is different from the previous knowledge we have explored so far in that it is an adjective while the others are verbs. An adjective is a word that describes a noun or a pronoun. It always has something that it is describing. An adjective may be demonstrative, descriptive, interrogative or possessive. This kind of knowledge therefore is that which describes or demonstrates a noun or a pronoun.

Ginosko for example, shows an action while gnostos knowledge describes or demonstrates what is known i.e. the substance. The book of Acts is usually also referred to as the 'book of action.' Little wonder gnostos appeared ten times in that book! This is a kind of knowledge that demonstrates what has happened. It is that kind of knowledge which makes available

112

to our human faculty occurred or occurring event. It is this kind of knowledge that God has made available to us through the exercise of our natural faculties, even in the absence of any supernatural revelation. By simply observing the physical universe which God has made, you can become aware (or gain knowledge of) the things that are made known through it.

"Because that which may be known (gnostos) of God is manifest in them; for God hath shewed [it] unto them. For the invisible things of him from the creation of the world are clearly seen, being understood by the things that are made, [even] his eternal power and Godhead; so that they are without excuse"

Romans 1:19-20

The above scriptures from verse 18 show that the anger of God is revealed from Heaven against the ungodliness and unrighteousness of men who are without excuse because God has made knowledge (gnostos) of Himself available to everyone. By merely observing the physical universe, we are being impacted or being made conscious of the existence of God. It would look quite silly to see people trying to explain creation through scientific evolution, stating that man came from something other than God and that God does not exist. If man came from monkeys then why do monkeys still exist? Well, I am yet to see the first monkey that will become a man someday! If you can lift up your eyes and explain what is above you and how it came into existence, you will realize that it is impossible to explain its existence without the workings and actions of a Supreme Being. This kind of knowledge in which God has made Himself knowable is gnostos, *"because that which is known (gnostos) about God is evident within them (us) for He made it evident to us."* (Romans 1:19).

Why is this kind of knowledge important? It is very important because it is the knowledge that gives insights into divine deeds intertwined with our surroundings and environment. It gives knowledge of God to the observer. For example, when a miracle takes place, the witnesses of this miracle are in possession of the knowledge of what has happened. This knowledge normally brings conviction. It convinces them and they have the fear of God and became aware that God is at work.

"Saying, what shall we do to these men? For that indeed a notable (gnostos) miracle hath been done by them is manifest to all them that dwell in Jerusalem; and we cannot deny it"

Acts 4:16

"And it was known (gnostos) throughout all Joppa; and many believed in the Lord"

Acts 9:42

There was an atmosphere of miracles surrounding Peter and John. They had notable miracles taking place all over. The environment was filled with gnostos knowledge (a known result). They couldn't deny the fact. Peter was filled with the Holy Ghost (Acts 4:8) and the atmosphere was charged with notable results, the fame of which spread abroad. Five thousand were added to the early church because as many people heard Peter speak they instantly believed (Acts 4:4). The ruler of the temple, the Sadducees, the high priests and many others gathered. They couldn't understand what kind of power was manifesting itself in the environment. They said to themselves that they have to stop Peter and John because their fame was increasing and many were being converted to Christ Jesus.

What was happening? A kind of knowledge (gnostos) was at work. It is a knowledge that demonstrates the person of Christ. It was a notable, evident knowledge. This knowledge describes something: an event, an atmosphere. The people had gnostos (were informed) or knew what occurred as a result of what they saw and heard. It had a greater influence in their lives yet the chief priests, the elders and the Sadducees still wanted to resist this power and knowledge at work. Peter rose up and said:

"Be it known (gnostos) unto you all and to all the people of Israel that by the name of Jesus Christ of Nazareth, whom ye crucified, whom God raised from the dead, even by him doth this man stand here before you whole"

Acts 4:10

He rose up and said *"men and brethren know (gnostos) that it is by the power of the Holy Ghost that this man is made whole"*. Gnostos knowledge is important because it is that kind of knowledge in which whenever a miracle occurs the people know that something has happened and they are convinced as a result of seeing it. When Jesus was on earth as a man, He performed many miracles, all of which were known (gnostos) to many, this is why people followed Him. He actually wanted people to know (gnostos) what was happening. It is the miracles and the wonders that help convince many to surrender to Him. If miracles weren't important, Jesus would not have wrought them. By the hands of Paul, God also wrought special miracles (Acts 19:11). I used to wonder why preachers who don't perform miracles criticize others who do. Men and brethren, miracles are important and needed. It is the occurrence of miracles that gives gnostos knowledge to their audiences and helps them to be convinced of the Jesus we preach. When miracles takes place, trepidation and awe falls on the people, many of whom are then convinced of God and His name is thus magnified.

"And this was known to all the Jews and Greeks also dwelling at Ephesus; and fear fell on them all, and the name of the Lord Jesus was magnified"

Acts 19:17

Dr T.L. Osborn explained how he and his wife went to China for missionary work and their mission was unfruitful. The Chinese practitioners would perform various types of miracles and people would follow those practitioners, but he was preaching Jesus Christ without any manifestation or proof. The environment was so tight. People had no gnostos knowledge of his miracles but rather the theoretical information. Later, he and his wife Daisy Osborn returned to U.S., where the encountered a man of God who changed their lives. The man of God expounded the Word of God to them and they were transformed. It seemed as though they have never read the Word of God before. They began applying the Word of God as real and raw as it is. Not long after, miracles started happening in their lives and ministry. They went back to China and India. Guess what? There was a turnaround in their ministry. They had evidence: their ministry became fruitful and is still yielding fruits till today. The people all around the cities knew that there was a God at work. It became known (gnostos) all over the world what God was using T.L. Osborn to do. His fame spread abroad! Men and brethren, miracles are necessary and I can say it is a must, for the sake of the Gospel.

The Transformative Power of the Gospel

People are tired of theories without practice. Information without impact changes neither a man nor a nation. It is the transformative information that has impact that can transform a man or a nation. The Word of God is not only information; it is that demonstrative and transformative information that bring transformation to every negative situation in a society. A society without the Word of God is unbalanced and deformed, thus revival is needed. A solid life and society is one whose foundation has in it the principles of the Kingdom: the Word of God. Without the spreading of this knowledge of God's Word, such a society is heading into demonism; i.e. a society in which demons control every aspect of it: the media, the government, the legislations, etc. Therefore, what will be the prevalent conditions in such a society? Poverty, abortions, murder, vandalism, homosexuality, etc. When God sent Jonah to Nineveh, He sent him to deliver the land from chaotic issues in the lives of its citizens by spreading the knowledge of God. When the Word of God grew in Ephesus it grew so mightily that it brought transformation. God wants people to know of Him. He wants to transform the nations through His Word. I pray that you will be a voice and a force of transformation as God uses you in your community. May the word of God in you not just stay in you but also overflow and bring change to the people around you. Gnostos is simply awareness generated through evidence.

The Divine Possibility Endowment

Are you familiar with the word antichrist? It is a compound word which stands for anti-against and Christ the anointed one. That means antichrist implies: against the Anointed One. Whosoever receives Christ becomes anointed!

"For as many of you as have been baptized into Christ have put on Christ"

Galatians 3:27

When you receive Christ you put on Christ. You put on the anointing of God and you are now the anointed of God. Every servant of God is the anointed of God. You are anointed with what I call a mandate possibility. The anointing is that oil that makes a God-given vision work. It can be called the divine possibility oil or endowment. The bible says, "Touch not my anointed." Not even in your mind or thoughts, not even in your bedroom. You are not supposed to be touched because you are the anointed king of God. He is the King of kings! Today I feel pity for such believers who ignorantly don't respect this instruction. They speak ill against the anointed ones of God. If you do this, you're a coworker with the antichrist. In fact, you are an antichrist if you touch the anointed one of God. Those who spend their entire life criticizing the anointed are simply the antichrist. You have no right to touch the Lord's anointed.

When God anoints you, it is for His work and His work is for His people. He has anointed you with the divine possibility endowment. He wants His people to feel that anointing, which is in and upon your life. He wants people to know that He is the Lord. He wants what He has done in the life of His anointed to be made known to others (gnostos). That is why in the bible there are records of history. What He did for others, He assures us through biblical history that He can do the same for us, even as He did for our father Abraham. He is the same yesterday, today tomorrow and forever more.

Therefore, know ye today that God is gloriously happy when knowledge of Him is known (gnostos) all over the society. He enjoys making Himself known to people. He also wants you to know Him by the actions He performs.

He is: *Jehovah- Rapha- the God your healer, Jehovah-Jireh- God your provider, Jehovah-Nissi- God of victory, etc.*

You see, even in His name He wants us to remember a particular revelation (knowledge) of Him. I can perhaps say that this knowledge (Gnostos) is also the knowledge of the present or past deeds of God. This knowledge describes and demonstrates Him as God in several domains. There is actually none like Him. He is in charge of your life and in charge of your entire family and loved ones. Go with this divine possibility oil in and upon you and spread the good news. Let everyone know of Him. " *Go in this thy might"*, He said!

Chapter 7

Gnosis Knowledge

The word gnosis is translated knowledge, doctrine, wisdom. It primarily means "a seeking to know, an enquiry, an investigation." It is a feminine noun which implies an experiential knowledge. It is knowledge gleaned from personal, firsthand experience. It is the knowledge that you as an individual acquire by investigation. It is the direct relationship between the spiritual and the physical worlds. This knowledge is available and accessible in the human realm via seeking, enquiring or investigating. It can also be referred to as a higher kind of intelligence and ability analogous to talent which is what Pluto used in his work Politikos, where he talked about one's aptitude.

It may also refer to a deep spiritual knowledge obtained through investigation or enquiries that can be expressed in the physical realm. Gnosis occurs about 29 times in the New

Testament and we are going to study some of the verses in which it appears in order to get a vital understanding of what gnosis really is. Gnosis signifies general intelligence. It is also translated as science (1 Timothy 6:20). It is a scientific knowledge and there are several forms of this knowledge. It may be knowledge of things or knowledge of God (Romans 11:33).

"Now I myself am confident concerning you, my brethren, that you also are full of goodness, filled with all knowledge, able also to admonish one another"

Romans 15:14

"That you were enriched in everything by Him in all utterance and all knowledge"

1 Corinthians 1:5

Just as there are various forms of knowledge, there can be good forms as well as evil or negative ones. The kind of knowledge that you pursue determines what you get. Gnosis knowledge is a deeper kind of knowledge about something or someone. Webster's dictionary defines this knowledge as: *"the deeper wisdom; knowledge of spiritual truth, such as was claimed by the Gnostics"*. It also adds: *"intuitive knowledge of spiritual truths"* and in Wikipedia *"gnosis signifies a spiritual knowledge, religion of knowledge, in the sense of mystical enlightenment or insight. It is often used for personal knowledge compared with intellectual knowledge (eidein), as with the French connaitre compared with savoir, or the German kennen rather than wissen"*

However, if you search the net you'll find several different definitions and interpretations of this knowledge - gnosis. Our aim here is to understand the biblical use of this word in order to derive the importance of it in our walk of faith and the body of Christ in general. For lack of knowledge kills and you can't get what you don't know. When you are aware of such knowledge it makes it palatable for you to go in search of what it reveals.

In 1 Timothy 6, Paul was encouraging Timothy to avoid certain disagreements and oppositions of knowledge. There he used the word science:

"O Timothy, keep that which is committed to thy trust, avoiding profane and vain babblings, and oppositions of science falsely so called: Which some professing have erred concerning the faith. Grace be with thee. Amen"

1 Timothy 6:20-21

In this verse where gnosis is translated as science, it has a negative meaning. This doesn't mean that science is something negative, no! It talks of avoiding oppositions of what is falsely called knowledge or science. Oh yes! We must avoid them. There are several people who tried to claim through various scientific knowledge that God doesn't exist. They try to explain scientific facts that appear to contradict the bible. Fact and reality such as the law of evolution or whatever theories there are, Paul by the Holy Spirit admonishes us to avoid them because they are falsely so called gnosis (sciences). Science or gnosis is not bad, but the motives or facts that are used to contradict scriptures, they are bad. The bible is the foundation of all knowledge. It should be the manual of every science because it contains all truth and facts that need to be known about life. It takes divine insight to extract and digest them. Before it was even proven that the earth is spherical the bible had already declared that and much more. Gnosis is a scientific knowledge implying an investigation, finding, or intelligence and it is something we need to press for and seek.

Daniel, Shadrach, Meshach and Abednego had this kind of knowledge. They were intelligent and divinely empowered to possess supernatural insight into reality. It is said of them:

"Children in whom was no blemish, but well favoured, and skilful in all wisdom, and cunning in knowledge (da'ath), and understanding science (madda'), and such as had ability in them to stand in the king's palace, and whom they might teach the learning and the tongue of the Chaldeans. As for these four children, God gave them knowledge (madda'), and skill in all learning

*and wisdom: and Daniel had understanding in
all visions and dreams"*

Daniel 1:4,17

Man! This knowledge is enough to govern, rule
and control any corporation and organization
on earth! Gnosis can beat down any foul play
on earth. These guys were blessed of God. This
knowledge comes from the Divine, or
supernatural realm. The world calls this
"mystical enlightenment or insight". It is God that
gives you this knowledge though the devil can
give you this knowledge as well but it will be
limited. Remember there were other people
such as the wise men, astrologers, interpreters
of dreams and magicians among the king's
nobles. Other people were also selected but
Daniel, Shadrach, Meshach and Abednego
were outstanding and ten times better.

*"And in all matters of wisdom and
understanding that the king enquired of them,
he found them ten times better than all the*

magicians and astrologers that were in all his realm"

Daniel 1:20

What an awesome God! This knowledge is available to anyone that seeks for he shall find and to anyone that ask unto God, He shall give it to him liberally that upbraideth not (James 1:5 paraphrased); but don't fold your arms and expect manna to fall from Heaven. You have "to seek", "to enquire", "to investigate" and even ask some questions.

Why would God give such knowledge to people? Why? Remember He gave them to rule, to lead and to disciple nations with it. He didn't give them to brag, no! He gave them to lead and be leaders in the land where they dwelled which by the way was a foreign land. The king was wise enough to seek such people who could stand in his appointed positions of leadership and government. If it was today's political leaders some would instead look for their relatives or connections etc. This knowledge is given to rule our world and to fulfill our calling here on earth. Therefore we all need gnosis.

Gnosis is one of the types of knowledge connected to human effort. It is an investigative or enquiring type of knowledge. It takes your cooperation to tap into it. You shouldn't just expect to wake up one morning and feel yourself impacted with gnosis. No laying of hands will give you this! It is a kind of knowledge that meets you at the level of findings, the room of consecration, the atmosphere of self-education and in the chambers of meditation. So, it has human effort and participation attached to it. We know that anything human has the potential to be fleshly. We can be tempted to brag about it. We can even be tempted to boast of it, hailing it as our achievements. It is this kind of knowledge the bible says *"knowledge puffs up"*.

"Now as touching things offered unto idols, we know that we all have knowledge. Knowledge puffeth up, but charity edifieth"

1 Corinthians 8:1

Note that it is not all kinds of knowledge that puff up; it is gnosis that puffs up; so don't go about concluding knowledge puffs up without first understanding the kind of knowledge the bible says puffed up. Epignosis for example, cannot cause one to be puffed up, because it is a divinely driven knowledge. It is not derived from our personal achievement; rather it draws us towards humility and takes us closer to God.

Another important thing to note here is that not all knowledge will pass away. It is gnosis that will pass away but epignosis cannot pass away because even in Heaven we will still be learning and knowing the beauty and splendor of our God. In Heaven for example when you see God, you won't need someone to introduce Him to you, you will just know without any protocol or teacher. This is a higher kind of knowing. This knowledge is epignosis. When you see Love, you'll know this is Love because you will experience and feel the reality of Love in your entire subconscious and conscious mind and in your spirit. In the spirit realm even after your physical death, there's a learning that still takes place. People who have had supernatural encounters or out of body and near dead experience often testify of things like this. It all involves a higher kind of knowledge greater than head knowledge.

"...whether there be knowledge (gnōsis), it shall vanish away"

1 Corinthians 13:8.

You won't be in the throne room of God starting to practice science or investigation, which is trying to know God using your intellectual knowledge. In Heaven, knowledge of Him will be imparted into your spirit. There you become what you know; you know something in its full reality. You know exactly as you are known, with all accuracy which our human vernacular cannot express. Heaven and earth shall pass away: there won't be need of this gnosis any more in the fullness of time. We only need this knowledge here and now on earth to take possession of that which has been freely given to mankind, believers or unbelievers alike.

It is impossible to fulfill your calling without being educated. Education is necessary and it has a vital part to play in your life here on earth. Speaking of education, I am not referring to certificates; I am referring to the education of the mind. The word educate comes from the Latin word *educo* which means to draw from within. Educating your brain enables you draw good treasures from within in order to use them in the affairs of life. Courses such as geology, meteorology etc. are discoveries made through gnosis knowledge. For example, it takes this kind of knowledge to land an object on Mars, for it involves diverse theories and researches made by many.

Just like ginosko, you can have gnosis in part or in full: i.e. knowledge of something in full. Gnosis is needed here on earth. We as a church are waiting to have the fullness of the knowledge (epignosis) of God. That's what we are driving towards daily, to come in the unity of the faith and the knowledge (epignosis) of the son of God unto a perfect man, unto the measure of the stature of the fullness of Christ, according to Ephesians 4:13, and to know the love of God which cannot be comprehended with our brain that surpasses gnosis knowledge. This is the Epignosis which we are going to look into in the last chapter of this book. It is that knowledge that drives us to know God's love and His fullness.

The Gift of the Word of Knowledge

I like the way Kenneth E. Hagin described this gift in his book entitled: *"The Holy Spirit and His Gifts"*. He said the gift of the word of knowledge is the supernatural revelation by the Holy Spirit of certain facts in the mind of God. It is not the "gift of knowledge" but the gift of "word of knowledge". It is a fragment of knowledge, it is not all knowledge imparted to an individual to know all things, rather it is simply a word of knowledge released into the spirit of an individual by the Holy Spirit. The word for knowledge used here is gnosis.

"Now concerning spiritual gifts, brethren, I would not have you ignorant. Now there are diversities of gifts, but the same Spirit. For to one is given by the Spirit the word of wisdom; to another the word of knowledge by the same Spirit; But all these worked that one and the selfsame Spirit, dividing to every man severally as he will"

1 Corinthians 12:1,4,8,11

Remember, the type of knowledge used here is gnosis which implies the gift of gnosis. This is a gift from the Holy Spirit that is a supernatural gift and it differs from natural gifts or endowments. There is natural head knowledge and there is supernatural knowledge. There is healing and there is the gift of healing, just as there is faith and there is also the gift of faith, etc. In natural healing, you can be healed through natural means and in supernatural healing, you are healed through the supernatural power of the Holy Spirit.

The gift of the word of knowledge is a supernatural impartation of gnosis. It gives

137

you present or past knowledge of something, be it visible or invisible, supernaturally, through the Holy Spirit. It is the Holy Ghost that imparts this knowledge into your human spirit and mind. Here, you possess an intellectual knowledge of something without any trace of human effort, influence, or even having studied the situation; for it's simply the Holy Ghost that gave you that knowledge. For example, you can know the formula to solve a mathematical question without having studied it anywhere. You can also know the root cause of a sickness and the history of a person without anyone telling you the story. This is the word of knowledge.

With the gift of the word of knowledge, it is difficult to answer the question "How did you know?" The how cannot be explained intellectually, such knowledge could only have come through the Holy Spirit. The Holy Spirit gave you certain facts from the mind of God: facts about people, places or things of the past or in the present moment. (Why? For the edification of His church and His people). In other words, it is a mental knowledge that came through the spiritual realm given by the Holy Spirit. There are several manifestations of this gift in the bible in both the new and old testaments.

In John chapter 4, when Jesus met the Samaritan woman, he said: *"The fact is, you have had five husbands, and the man you now have is not your husband. What you have just said is quite true"*(John 4:18). How did Jesus know the exactitude of this situation? It was through the Holy Spirit.

Also, in the old testament when the donkey of Saul's father was lost (1 Samuel 9), he went in search of it. It was proving quite difficult to trace and locate the donkey. They had to go and meet Prophet Samuel who later unfolded to them the location and everything about the donkey. That was the word of knowledge in operation. The word of knowledge is not limited to spiritual things only. It is the knowledge of physical things given by the Holy Spirit; so it is a gift given to provide benefits in both physical and spiritual matters.

"But the manifestation of the Spirit is given to every man to profit withal"

1 Corinthians 12:7

A lot of people in churches nowadays simply manifest this gift to tell people of how many demons they have and which witchcraft is pursuing their lives, No! Go beyond that. Through this gift you can advise the government of your country how to restructure its leadership. Just like Elisha (2 Kings 6:12), you can reveal terrorists attack and strategies to combat them.

I read the story of an engineer who, when faced with difficult situations or projects, would simply asked his workers to give him a few minutes. He would go and pray, speak in tongues then return with detail plans and ideas of how the project needed to be executed. However, do bear in mind that the Holy Spirit has diverse ways to manifest this gift in our lives.

Jacob, when he was cheated by Laban, did something fascinating that is difficult to comprehend on a mortal level. He came up with a scientific combination of crossbreeding that proved superior to the knowledge of his opponent. Let's see what he did:

"Now it came about when Rachel had borne Joseph that Jacob said to Laban, "Send me away, that I may go to my own place and to my own country. Give me my wives and my children for whom I have served you, and let me depart; for you yourself know my service which I have rendered you." But Laban said to him, "If now it pleases you, stay with me; I have divined that the Lord has blessed me on your account." He continued, "Name me your wages, and I will give it." But he said to him, "You yourself know how I have served you and how your cattle have fared with me. For you had little before I came and it has increased to a multitude, and the Lord has blessed you wherever I turned. But now, when shall I provide for my own household also?" So he said, "What shall I give you?" And Jacob said, "You shall not give me anything. If you will do this one thing for me, I will again pasture and keep your flock: let me pass through your entire flock today, removing from

there every speckled and spotted sheep and every black one among the lambs and the spotted and speckled among the goats; and such shall be my wages. So my honesty will answer for me later, when you come concerning my wages. Every one that is not speckled and spotted among the goats and black among the lambs, if found with me, will be considered stolen." Laban said, "Good, let it be according to your word." So he removed on that day the striped and spotted male goats and all the speckled and spotted female goats, everyone with white in it, and all the black ones among the sheep, and gave them into the care of his sons. And he put a distance of three days' journey between himself and Jacob, and Jacob fed the rest of Laban's flocks.

Then Jacob took fresh rods of poplar and almond and plane trees, and peeled white stripes in them, exposing the white which was in the rods. He set the rods which he had peeled in front of the flocks in the gutters, even in the watering troughs, where the flocks came to drink; and they mated when they came to drink. So the flocks mated by the rods, and the flocks brought forth striped, speckled, and spotted. Jacob separated the lambs, and made the flocks face toward the striped and all the black in the flock of Laban; and he put his own herds apart, and did not put them with Laban's flock. Moreover, whenever the stronger of the flock were mating, Jacob would place the rods in the sight of the flock in the gutters, so that they might mate by the rods; but when the flock was feeble, he did not put them in; so the feebler were Laban's and the stronger Jacob's. So the man became exceedingly prosperous, and had large flocks and female and male servants and camels and donkeys"

Genesis 30:25-43

Until now science cannot comprehend this; and that is why some have concluded that the bible has errors. Let me make it clear to you: you cannot explain *the how* of spiritual things. When God gives you the gift of the word of gnosis (knowledge), it is difficult to fathom how you know whatever you know or will know. You should note that it is a gift that operates only through the influence of the Holy Spirit. This gift is given to you not as your personal property that you can just switch on any time you want. No, it is the Holy Spirit that activates it any time He wants.

Bear in mind though, that you are meant to desire this spiritual gift so that you might profit thereby. God has plans to bless you and to prosper you. He wants to make you exceedingly great and full of knowledge. He is the all-knowing God: He has all knowledge and that's why He wants to impact your life with this knowledge so that you may be equipped to fulfill your purpose here on earth. He sent you here for a mission and without a vision which involves knowledge you will perish. This knowledge will teach you how to go about executing your projects in this life. Desire this gift!

"Follow after charity and desire spiritual gifts.... Even so ye forasmuch as ye are zealous of spiritual gifts seek, that ye may excel to the edifying of the church"

1 Corinthians 14:1,12

The Power of the Soul

Gnosis is that knowledge for which you enquire, you seek and you research. It actually has a link to the invisible realm of man. The invisible realm is the realm of the spirit and the soul of man. This realm is endowed with power from on high. Your soul comprises of your mind, your emotions and your will. It has been created by God and possesses natural ability to do marvelous things in the earth realm. It is a kind of middle-man between your spirit and your body. Your spirit is the habitat of God and enables you to communicate with divinity. The soul receives information or knowledge from both the spirit and the body. Your body is the carrier of both your soul and spirit. It relates or links you to this material world. To be dead only refers to the body without the spirit as explained in James 1:26. Your body sends information to your soul through the five senses and your soul receives this information and processes it. Also, your spirit sends information to your soul which it also digests. The real you is your spirit-man while your soul-man is the center of procession of information from your spirit and body. When you talk of self consciousness and self control, you are referring to the soul, which is the part of you that Jesus came to save and needs to be transformed by the Word. Your spirit is of God and will go back to God and body of the earth and it will go back to dust (Ecclesiastes 12:7).

You now as the soul have two sources of information, that of your spirit and that from the body which is the earthly man. (But you have to note that there's a connection among the three). You can receive as an example 90% of information from the spirit man and 10% from the earthly man. We as believers of Jesus Christ have been taught not to be led by the things of the world that is the outer man. The things of the world are temporal and do not know the world in it's entirely; meanwhile, the spirit man knows the world and even that which is in the mind of God. God can unleash the secrets of the world to us and help direct our lives through the spirit man. Sometimes

God really wants to direct us but there is a hindrance in the soul. This hindrance might be placed by information that we accessed from the world. For us to enter the kingdom of God, we have to become like little babies. Why? Because they have a pure soul, that is to say they are innocent because the world hasn't passed information into their soul or mind yet. They are more of spiritual beings and can easily make it to heaven. As they grow (if not well directed), they become much more self conscious (rather than spirit conscious) and most of the information received comes from the physical world which then hinders or even stops the flow of information coming from their inner man - the spirit (the real man).

When we come to that stage, the age of awareness, we are supposed to get born again and repent of our sins. Now as born again believers all that is required of us is to be transformed by the renewing of our minds. This transformation shifts us from being self conscious to being God conscious and enables us to have dominion over our soul, thereby controlling our thoughts, emotions, will, etc. In this way, we talk of self control which is the fruit our inner man now produces.

"And be not conformed to this world: but be ye transformed by the renewing of your mind, that ye may prove what is that good, and acceptable, and perfect, will of God"

Romans 12:2

So our mind which is in the soul needs transformation. This transformation has to come through knowledge, which is gnosis. We have to grow in this knowledge of God and the precepts of life.

"...grow in grace, and in the knowledge (gnosis) of our Lord and Saviour Jesus Christ"

2 Peter 3:18

We have to grow and be transformed. Our transformation is a by-product of our will and effort. It is not God that will transform you, for you are responsible for your transformation. You transform yourself by the information you acquire and the environment you create for yourself. Man has will power which has been given to him by God. Neither God nor the devil can violate your will. Therefore, the ball is in your court, you determine whether or not you wish to grow in knowledge and enjoy the life and liberty provided for you by God. Your transformation is a by-product of the effort and ability you put in.

The Power of Labor

This knowledge doesn't just come overnight. It doesn't come by chance; it takes several efforts and collaboration for you to possess this knowledge. You have to labor for it. Everything on earth is made available for man to acquire knowledge of it, but that knowledge has been concealed. It is the glory of a king to search out that knowledge and to get a hold of it. Even animals find more pleasure in eating prey that they labored for. Nature is made in a way that satisfaction comes after sacrifice. It is your sacrifice that gives you satisfaction. For nature to favor you, you have to labor, for labor is the platform for favor. There is actually no gain without pain. You have to apply the pain of discipline in order for you to escape the pain of regret. We normally say you've got to sweat to get the sweet. Perhaps you want to be intelligent, lose weight, stay healthy, fulfill your purpose, etc. it will take labor for you to accomplish that. God created man to stay in the garden and cater for it. Not to relax and wait for fruits of the garden to come, No! If you violate this law of nature, you simply give room for mediocrity.

"Let us labor therefore to enter into that rest"

Hebrews 4:11

There is a rest for the people of God. All we need in order to enter into it is labor. God does not just bless us; rather He blesses the works of our hands. Work is the application of force. An object will remain in a constant state which is equivalent to being dead if force is not applied to it. Dead things don't move, faith is dead unless work is applied to it. Rarely do you find a constant life or thing remaining in a good state. You either decrease or increase in value. For example, if you travel and leave your room for about 6 years without anyone touching it, you'll come back and find it deteriorating even when everything was in a constant state. Labor can change your life. Therefore brethren, change your lives through labor!

The Power of Concentration

Man's supernatural energy is released when there is great concentration. There is power in concentration. When the rays of light are concentrated, it can split whatever substance that has been its focus. A scattered ray is powerless and lack impact. You can't feel the effect of such light rays. Concentration harmonizes the power in you for a tremendous result. It helps you to focus all your energy on a particular task. It brings unity between your body, soul and spirit and then releases its energy or focus on a particular task for its accomplishment. "If two shall agree as touching anything, it shall be established"

Wherever you are and whatever you are doing, if there is no concentration your work will be fruitless. I have never seen a great man with a great result and great invention without concentration. Concentration causes you to be highly effective. Exactly as a highly concentrated laser beam can shrivel an object that is the same way you release and achieve great results through concentration. The devil wants you to be busied with nothing and when you are busy you'll hardly find time to focus on a particular task. A lot of people can hardly stand to be alone and focus on a particular task; they would rather look for people to talk to and things to keep themselves distracted by either watching movies or surfing the net. Don't let your mind roam on things, learn to concentrate, focus on the goal you want to achieve and you will achieve it. Be careful for nothing. Worrying is one of the disease that can take you off your concentration and thus deprive you of your creative ability which is released during concentration. Concentration also enables you to develop a quiet and calm spirit.

The Power of Imagination

In the pursuit of insight or knowledge, imagination is inescapable. Imagination is forming a mental image of that which may not be perceived through our senses. It helps to make knowledge applicable in solving problems relating to your calling. It gives you the ability to explore ideas of things that are not yet available in our physical environment. Knowledge is impossible without the ability to imagine. You can grab a hold of anything if you can look beyond your present environment. Imagination is one of the tools that brings the invisible into the visible realm. You shouldn't quench your imagination; rather create a conducive environment that will develop your imagination. Also, a child limited in imagination is likely to have a limited knowledge and thus a limited future. To change the future generation, we have to first change their thinking! If we don't do it purposely, the media would help us do it indirectly. Let your child and yourself think big, way beyond your present environment. In the book of Genesis God promised Abraham a child, but many years went by yet the child did not come. Eventually God called Abraham and showed him the stars. He said: *"Look at the stars. If indeed you can count them...."* then he said to him: *"so shall your offspring be"* (Gen. 15:5). This alone gave him the picture of the future. As he looked at the stars, he got a dream! That picture transmitted information into his subconscious mind which gave him the ability to line up his thought with God's plan and thus enabled him to accomplished God's plan for his life.

Knowledge is impossible without imagination. Another instance of this occurred in Genesis 11, when the people wanted to build a tower that would touch Heaven but God stopped them. God's response actually astonishes me. He said *".... Now nothing will be withheld from them which they have imagined to do"*.

"Whatever your mind can conceive and believe, it can achieve." Napoleon Hill.

The Power of Motivation

Motivation is not just a message, it is a push factor. It is an empowerment. You will never achieve anything if you're not motivated towards it! Your energy becomes greater when you're motivated from within or without. Discouragement is simply a lack of motivation. Lack of motivation is the absence of momentum towards an object or goal. There are many sources of motivation: we can either be spiritually or physically motivated. You keep doing what you are doing because you're motivated to do it.

I have never achieved anything without motivation. I could not have written this book without motivation. Your motivation determines your action and keeps you moving. You can't possess knowledge without motivation. For you to excel in your field or sphere of influence you need knowledge and your pursuit of knowledge come through motivation. There are some friends that I like being around as it becomes an instrument of motivation for me, meanwhile there are others

I don't like being around because they are like fire extinguishers. After a meeting with them, it's either I find myself broken, discouraged or lukewarm. The latter are the categories of people who kill visions and keep you in total frustration. Therefore, when it comes to motivation, your circle of friends and environments have a great role to play in it. We all need motivation, for it brings challenge. It can also create an environment for positive competition which sets the pace for action. Motivation is not a one-time event; it is something you must seek continuously and frequently. Zig Ziglar said: "People often say that motivation doesn't last. Well, neither does bathing- that's why we recommend it daily." I would prefer to be alone than to be with friends who kill my zeal. Pursue motivation, for it is a prerequisite for the acquisition of knowledge.

The Power of Mentorship

Another factor to put in place in the pursuit of gnosis is mentorship. What is mentorship? It is simply following the steps of those who have gone ahead of you. It is learning from the experience of more knowledgeable people. Mentorship is discipleship: it is being disciple by someone as you move towards the fulfillment of your life purpose. It can be academic, spiritual, professional, marital mentorship etc. Mentorship involves your will. There must be a willingness to be mentored accompanied by deliberate submission of your will in order to progress in a particular sphere or direction. You must earnestly desire it and be willing to be mentored. No one is *all knowing* except God for He is the all wise God. We have to learn from others, nothing is actually new on the earth today. Someone laid the foundation in previous years for everything that is being discovered today. Those who have lived before simply laid the foundation for us to lay ours on and then pass it on to the next generation. The generation that succeeds us shall lay theirs on what this generation has laid already. Even the first person who went to the moon was able to do so using the knowledge of others even though they had never been there before. You see? Mentorship is learning from others in order for us to go further. Through mentorship, one is able to sustain a lifetime legacy of knowledge by receiving (as a mentee) and transferring (as a mentor) to the next generation. We can be mentored through books, CDs, videos etc. It can also be achieved through formal or informal education. In the bible no one just appeared independently, No! They all had a reference point. Who is your reference?

Madda Knowledge

In the Old Testament, the bible makes mention of Solomon and Daniel being filled with wisdom and knowledge from the Lord. Solomon wasn't just filled with wisdom; he was filled with wisdom and knowledge. This knowledge in Hebrew is madda which is translated in the book of Daniel as understanding science. It occurs only six times in the Old Testament addressing Solomon, Daniel and the three Hebrew boys. Of Daniel and his friends the bible says that they were:

"...handsome and skillful in all wisdom and in knowledge (da'ath), and understanding science (madda)... As for these four children, God gave them knowledge (madda) and skill in all learning and wisdom"

Daniel 1:4,17

Why would God give anyone this knowledge? This knowledge was usually given for national leadership and oversight of countries. The scripture tells us that God created man to be fruitful, multiply, replenish, have dominion and to rule. This was a leadership responsibility in man's domain of influence. Therefore Daniel, Shadrach, Meshach and Abednego had this knowledge to rule and take dominion over the affairs of life. They were leaders with outstanding results. They had the ability to dissolve doubt and crack hard problems such as riddles, because there was an excellent spirit from God in them.

"Forasmuch as an excellent spirit, and knowledge, and understanding, interpreting of dreams, and shewing of hard sentences, and dissolving of doubts, were found in the same Daniel, whom the king named Belteshazzar: now let Daniel be called, and he will shew the interpretation"

Daniel 5:12

This knowledge that brought an outstanding result in them came as a result of an excellent Spirit from above, not from beneath. The situation seems contrary today; some world leaders would prefer to go and search for knowledge and powers from the wrong source, i.e. from the world beneath and not from above. No doubt you'll find that many of them belong to different cult groups and so on. They are searching for that which will make them outstanding in their positions of leadership. Outstanding results and knowledge that brings protection only come from above and not from beneath. Note that anything that is above is above all.

Let us look at Solomon in the scripture when he was made king: when God asked him what he wanted, he requested wisdom and knowledge (madda).

"And Solomon said unto God, Thou hast shewed great mercy unto David my father, and hast made me to reign in his stead. Give me now wisdom and knowledge that I may go out and come in before this people: for who can judge this thy people that is so great? And God said to Solomon, Because this was in thine heart, and thou hast not asked riches, wealth, or honour, nor the life of thine enemies, neither yet hast asked long life; but hast asked wisdom and knowledge for thyself, that thou mayest judge my people, over whom I have made thee king"

2 Chronicles 1:8,10,11

Solomon didn't just ask for wisdom alone, he asked for this deep knowledge from above. To reign in this life you need gnosis or madda.

161

Gnosis is God's will for you. He is the one that gives you this knowledge. The devil can also give you knowledge and wisdom but it is all from beneath and it is likely that you will have to pay back. Gnosis knowledge is available and we can all tap into that realm. Many great brain scientists that we know of today had access to this kind of knowledge. People like Albert Einstein, Thomas Edison, Isaac Newton and even modern day scientists have all laid hold of deeper knowledge. Most of them had links to one spiritual root or another. They had a spiritual lifestyle irrespective of what source it was. You need to be spiritual in order to make it in this life! This knowledge is available for spiritual people: I urge you to go for that knowledge that comes from above, that knowledge that Solomon went for in prayer, that knowledge that Daniel had which made him ten times better. That knowledge is available for the church today. The body of Christ needs this knowledge and God is willing and faithful to give it to anyone who seeks it.

My prayer for you dear reader, is that God will impact your life, ministry and career with gnosis and madda, knowledge from above. I decree that you shall be outstanding in your sphere of influence. I decree that you will be able to dissolve doubts and dilute every tough challenge; people will identify you as filled with the knowledge of God.

Chapter 8

Epignosis Knowledge

Having looked into the other kinds of knowledge, epignosis is the final type of knowledge that we are going to examine in this book. It is the most needed knowledge in the body of Christ.

Epignosis is a compound word: epi and gnosis. Epi is advanced and deeper while gnosis is the knowledge already discussed in the previous chapter. Epignosis comes from the word group gnosis. It refers to deeper, intimate, experiential knowledge. Epignosis is a noun and epiginosko is the verb. In a sense, epignosis is a substance. There is epignosis of God, of Christ, of the truth or the blessing set upon us. The bible speaks of the epignosis of God: Christ, the epignosis of the will of the Lord, the mystery of God. (Ephesians 4:13)

Epignosis is exact or full knowledge. It expresses a greater participation by the knower in the subject known. It powerfully influences the knower so when you have the epignosis of something you have a greater involvement with that thing. It is a more strengthened form of ginosko-knowledge. You can have ginosko knowledge of God and yet the fruit of godliness is not seen in you, but you can't have epignosis of God without bearing fruit. Epignosis is actually the knowledge that gives you access to everything pertaining to life and godliness.

The book of Romans talks about a set of believers with ginosko knowledge of God but without epignosis of God; or, they refused to possess epignosis of God and as a result they were given over to vile affections and fleshly lust.

"For the wrath of God is revealed from heaven against all ungodliness and unrighteousness of men, who hold the truth in unrighteousness; Because that which may be known of God is manifest in them; for God hath shewed it unto them. For the invisible things of him from the creation of the world are clearly seen, being understood by the things that are made, even

his eternal power and Godhead; so that they are without excuse: Because that, when they knew God, they glorified him not as God, neither were thankful; but became vain in their imaginations, and their foolish heart was darkened. For this cause God gave them up unto vile affections: for even their women did change the natural use into that which is against nature: And likewise also the men, leaving the natural use of the woman, burned in their lust one toward another; men with men working that which is unseemly, and receiving in themselves that recompence of their error which was meet. And even as they did not like to retain God in their knowledge, God gave them over to a reprobate mind, to do those things which are not convenient;"

Romans 1:18-21, 26-28.

If you read the entire chapter of Romans 1, you will realize that this people established a relationship with God but they refused to go further (epi). They remained at ginosko-knowledge; but think about this, why did Jesus come? Why are we preaching? What is the mission or purpose of the church? It is:

"... all men to be saved and to come unto the knowledge of the truth"

1 Timothy 2:4

God wants every man to come to a higher knowledge of the truth. A kind of knowledge where you not only profess the truth but you participate in the truth and the truth influences you then you become the exactitude of what you know. You become a substance of the thing or object you know. The scripture says we shall know even as we are known (1 Corinthians 13:12). You know as you know yourself. Here you participate and know fully and exactly, not partially but in full. Have you ever seen a patient trying to explain his/her situation to the doctor? Only then does the doctor try to understand and prescribe drugs according to his understanding. The patient knows the specificity of the pain. Only the victim has the precise understanding of the experienced pain and he/she can't fully

167

transmit the experience of that pain to the third party. This is the case when one has experiential knowledge of an object. Epignosis is an experienced knowledge whereby you participate in the object known. Experience is the best teacher. When you experience something or have an encounter, you alone know the impact of the experience. God wants all believers to grow and to come to the full, exact, experiential knowledge of the truth, His personality and His will.

Access to Divine Truth

Many of the promises of God still remain mental knowledge in believers' lives. Your profitability from the Word will only come when you convert mental assent to actual reality. That is why mediating on the Word of God must have a place in our lives. It plays a convectional role. Many years ago, I had the head knowledge of the divine healing but the day the Word of God came alive in my spirit concerning healing, man! It was so real;

without a doubt I leapt out of the bed of sickness, never to return till Jesus comes. But before then, guess what? I had all the excuses to give: "You know, this and that blah, blah, blah." Brethren, the day you encounter or experience truth, all mental knowledge will dissipate and you will be what the scripture says you are. When God says you're rich, you're the head and not the tail, He means what He said. Epignosis is that knowledge that will enable us become the thing we know, meanwhile mental knowledge gives us the awareness. It awakens that consciousness in us. Some people get tired of God along the way; some succumb to satanic spirits and conclude that the Word of God doesn't work. They have not reached epignosis; they are trying to understand God with head knowledge. Your head cannot comprehend the fabulous, gracious mercy and love of God. You need an encounter, you need an experience. People of God perish not because God doesn't want to save them but simply because they lack this experiential knowledge. Your access to divine truth will come through epignosis.

"According as his divine power hath given unto us all things that pertain unto life and godliness, through the knowledge of him that hath called us to glory and virtue"

2 Peter 1:3

Access to things that pertain to life such as health, wealth, strength and things that pertain to godliness such as joyfulness, holiness, righteousness, etc. only come through epignosis of God. True, the scripture says if any man is in Christ He is a new creation; old things have passed away…. (2 Corinthians 5:17 paraphrased), but when you become a new man spiritually, your new man only becomes evident through epignosis.

"And have put on the new man, which is renewed in knowledge (epignosis) after the image of him that created him"

Colossians 3:10

The new man is the one that walks in the similitude of Christ. You look into Christ and you become transformed into His image. When you look into the scripture, epignosis gives you the knowledge that transforms you to become what is written of you. You become the Christ. You lose your own identity and through this knowledge, you become Christ. The life that you live in the flesh is no longer you that lives but it is Christ that lives in you. Without epignosis all these things are fairy tales or a mere philosophy, theosophy or mythology. We are actually called by God to reveal the image and person of Him who called us. He called us to be His ambassadors; to be like Him. He says "... *as He is, so are we in this world*" (1 John 4:17), because his love has been made perfect in us. You must become it in the same sense as you become Him. When men look at you in reality, they know that they have seen Christ in you. You become the exact image of Christ.

Now how many believers are at this stage? We grow in knowledge to enter in this phase of life. Growth never ends; God wants us to come to that stage of completion. This is one of the reasons He placed apostles, prophets, evangelists, pastors and teachers in the church, to perfect the saints till we all come to the unity of faith and to the epignosis of God, as it is written:

"For the perfecting of the saints, for the work of the ministry, for the edifying of the body of Christ: Till we all come in the unity of the faith, and of the knowledge-epignosis of the Son of God, unto a perfect man, unto the measure of the stature of the fullness of Christ"

Ephesians 4:12-13

Hallelujah! Therefore it is possible to be a perfect man and having the fullness of Christ. This is possible through growth and increase in epignosis knowledge. This is the kind of person of whom the scriptures says: *"Whoever is born of God doesn't commit sin...he cannot sin because he is born of God." **1 John 3:9**.* It really means you can't commit sin. Well, some ministers of the gospel can't believe this and as a result they have given different explanations to contradict the context of this verse. Cannot commit sin means cannot commit sin! Now it's not everyone that can not commit sin. It takes growth; that's to say; you are growing and moving progressively towards the place where you are totally sinless, to where sin can never be identified in you. We're moving to the place of perfectness, unity of faith and the epignosis of our God!

"And have put on the new man, which is renewed in knowledge after the image of him that created him"

Colossians 3:10

You become Christ, which is the righteousness of God in reality not only spiritually but physically as well. Here you become the epitome of love and righteousness. Have you ever imagined touching the physical hands of Jesus? By simply looking at Jesus you can feel and sense his righteousness, you can feel the highest kind of love, one which you have never experienced before. If He opens his mouth and tells you, *"Son, I love you."* you will see yourself engulfed in that love instantly. His words give you the experience and expression of what is said. It acts like the rhema word of God whereby you feel the weight and the substance of the word.

Impossible to Sin

After acquiring the epignosis of God, it becomes impossible for you to sin or for you to turn back from God. You become one with Him. Most people who backslide from the faith haven't actually made it to this stage. I strongly believe there are few believers that have attained this similitude state. Most people only confess it. Of course that is also good as it is the pathway to becoming what you are confessing.

Epignosis gives you access to heavenly treasures. You become part of the Holy Ghost and taste the heavenly gift and the powers of the world to come. The scriptures teach us that with this kind of knowledge sin becomes impossible because sinning is like returning to one's own vomit. No man in his right mind will even think of doing that. Furthermore, the bible describes willful sin as actually crucifying Christ a second time. You are like Christ! You definitely cannot afford to crucify him! This is the experiencing of knowledge, partaking of it. It is becoming what you are coming to know. This of course is far more than head knowledge.

"For it is impossible for those who were once enlightened, and have tasted of the heavenly gift, and were made partakers of the Holy Ghost, And have tasted the good word of God, and the powers of the world to come, If they shall fall away, to renew them again unto repentance; seeing they crucify to themselves the Son of God afresh, and put him to an open shame"

Hebrews 6:4-6

It is impossible to renew them again unto repentance. Yeah! The bible says it is impossible! No! Don't say that is not what it meant that it wasn't accurately translated. Sometimes when people's head knowledge can't fully grasp what the bible says by simply taking the word as it is, they try to explain it to fit their own theology. If only we could take the Word of God the way it is, the Holy Ghost would then be able to help us fully digest whatever it said about us. Remember, when you take God at His word you'll have the result! The above verse was correctly translated and what it says is exactly what is meant. Impossible to renew them again unto repentance again! Why? Now, let us take the case of an angel because they are equivalent to this kind of person just that this one is a little lower. If for example the angel Gabriel was to come to earth and commit fornication with a lady, do you think he would just say *"God forgive me and wash my sin with the blood of Jesus and take me back to heaven."*? No! He would not even have a place in Heaven any more. He would be like other fallen angels who sinned against God and were cast down with Lucifer. On the other hand, it is impossible for Gabriel to even have an iota of thought about sinning. This is because; he is a created and complete spirit being who dwells in the presence of God. He is a partaker of the heavenly host and divine presence. He has seen and experienced in a real sense the splendor and beauty of the glory of God. Even when he carries a message from God, He doesn't only carry the letters but he carries the power and authority that backed the message. When he speaks, you feel like it is God speaking to you directly. You feel that tenacity of power and glory and the light that flows from the throne room of God. The light that radiates his mind is enough to eliminate darkness. He can't sin, even though he has the power to but he can't, not to talk of sinful imaginations. It is impossible! He has the epignosis knowledge of God in full and cannot even imagine the contrary. He has come to the full knowledge of the truth and has overrides the flesh. He is more of a spirit than humans.

"For if after they have escaped the pollutions of the world through the knowledge of the Lord and Saviour Jesus Christ, they are again entangled therein, and overcome, the latter end is worse with them than the beginning"

2 Peter 2:20

"For if we sin wilfully after that we have received the knowledge-epignosis of the truth, there remaineth no more sacrifice for sins"

Hebrews 10:26

After we have successfully escaped the defilement of this word through epignosis of Jesus Christ and decide to sin willfully, there remains no more sacrifice of sins. This is referring to a higher rank; not just any kind of Christian. There is no getting out of the truth of this scripture. It is what it is.

Needless to say, we are not to go and meet a choir director who committed sin and say: *"Oh no! You've received epignosis of God already. There is therefore no more sacrifice of sin for you. You have committed the unpardonable sin. Oh no! You won't be forgiven."* That is condemnation and judgment. Only the devil is expected to do that. Someone with epignosis won't even think of committing a sin, for he is the embodiment of Christ in an earthen vessel.

The Unpardonable Sin

What is the unpardonable sin? Can we commit the unpardonable sin? Yes! The unpardonable sin is not any of the much spoken of sins like fornication or adultery like David would have been an example of if that were the case, or the sin of lying like Abraham who lied by saying that Sarah was his sister would have been a victim, or unbelief like doubting Thomas who saw Jesus in both human and glorified form would have committed. Many of us who sometimes doubt God's promises and walk in unbelief would have committed it as well if it were such a sin. For whatever is not done of faith is sin. It is a sin that can be committed only by a certain group of people. Rarely would you find Christians who have committed this sin. For you to commit this sin you must have attained full maturity and received epignosis of Christ.

The unpardonable sin therefore, is when a mature believer rejects the Holy Spirit. He rejects the person of Christ after having known him fully well. Kenneth E. Hagin listed five qualities the scripture says a person must have had in order to be able to fulfill. They are:

- You must have been enlightened.

- You must have tasted the heavenly gift, which refers to accepting the person of Jesus, for he is the gift of God.

- Partaking or sharing with the Holy Spirit which means having an infilling presence of the Holy Ghost.

- Partaking and tasting the good word of God.

- Partaking of the power of the world to come.

Here you become partakers of heavenly things. Being part of such an experience it's unimaginable that such a person could even think of going back to the world. If you do, however, the scripture says: *"For it had been better for them not to have known the way of righteousness, than after they have known it, to turn from the Holy commandment delivered unto them."* (2 peter 2:21).

The Christian journey is a race. We are heading somewhere; we are driving to get to the place of full knowledge of the things we seek. Epiginosko is the way, the action step, towards the end result which is the place of completion and full knowledge. We are heading to the epignosis of God and Christ, to the epignosis of the will of God, to the epignosis of every good thing given to us, the epignosis of the truth, the epignosis of the mystery of God (Colossians 2:2) and the epignosis of knowledge of all things. (Philippians 1:9)

Seven Required Qualities for the Epignosis of the Lord Jesus Christ

Since epignosis is not just an instant occurrence, there are some qualities which are prerequisites to its attainment. The bible mentions these qualities and says, *"for if these things be in you and abound, they make you that ye shall neither be barren nor unfruitful in the knowledge-epignosis of our Lord Jesus Christ"* (2 Peter 1:8). What are these qualities that will make us neither barren nor unfruitful in the epignosis of our Lord? Reading from verse 3 to 28 of 2nd Peter, all these qualities are mentioned. In my book *"The Four Dimensions Of the Word of God"*, I also mentioned these qualities. They are as follows:

1. *"And beside this, giving all diligence, add to your faith virtue"*

In other words, it says make haste to add to your faith virtue or moral excellence. It is talking to fathers who already posses ginosko knowledge. It says we, not God, should add virtue to our faith. We already have some measure of faith. We live by the faith of Christ's love for us (Galatians 2:20). It is our duty to add virtue or moral excellence to our faith in our walk with God. If we lack this, the Bible says we shall stumble, but if it be in us and if it abounds, then not only will we conquer but our environment will be affected also.

2. *"And to virtue knowledge"*

We are to add knowledge to virtue. The knowledge here is gnosis. Since epignosis is advance gnosis you can't have epignosis without gnosis. We as Christians are to be examples of moral excellence in any environment that we find ourselves. We are the ideal personality our community needs. It is also necessary for us to be intelligent and possess a deeper understanding of our Christian walk. Therefore, to obtain epignosis, you also need intelligent or head knowledge.

3. *"And to knowledge (gnosis), temperament (or self control)"*

If you can't say no to yourself, you will be controlled by everything around you. Have you realized that one of the most difficult things to say is "No"? When it is time to pray, study or meditate, we should endeavor to say no to laziness or sleep. People are free to interrupt our schedules as they like if we are not masters of ourselves. We need to be disciplined! Self control is a fruit of a regenerated spirit. It puts the focus on what you want to achieve in life.

4.   *"And to temperance, patience"*

Lack of patience is one of the reasons why many have lost their faith. They are so impatient that when they pray and do not get instant results, they conclude that God doesn't answer their prayers. If only we would be patient, we would truly depend on God and as such, we would win in life. *"In your patience possess ye your souls"* Luke 21:19

5.   *"And to patience, godliness"*

The word godliness here also means reverence, respect and holiness. We are commanded to be holy; we are to respect one another. Without holiness we cannot see God. The righteousness of God has been imparted to us; therefore we have to strive to be holy as our father is Holy (1 Peter 1:16)

6.   "And   to   godliness   brotherly kindness"

This is the Greek word philadelphia (from *philos,* "loving friend" and *adelphós,* "a brother") which means brotherly love. To be in full possession of epignosis of God, we need to be transformed into the image of Christ. Our Christianity should not only be centered on our family and ourselves; we need to extend God's love to those around us. We shouldn't be egocentric.

7.   "And to brotherly kindness charity"

The Greek word used here is agape - the love of God. *The love of God has been shed abroad in our heart (Romans 5:5).* We ought to act or be doers of this love. We should manifest love. The love of God knows no evil, it is unconditional. You just love as Christ loves the church. Love your environment whether it is good or not. Agape has no reason or condition, it just loves.

"For if you possess these qualities in increasing measure, they will keep you from being ineffective and unproductive in your knowledge of our Lord Jesus Christ
But whoever does not have them is nearsighted and blind, forgetting that they have been cleansed from their past sins.
Therefore, my brothers and sisters, make every effort to confirm your calling and election.
For if you do these things, you will never stumble, and you will receive a rich welcome into the eternal Kingdom of our Lord and Savior Jesus Christ. So I will always remind you of these things, even though you know them and are firmly established in the truth you now have.
I think it is right to refresh your memory as long as I live in the tent of this body"

2 Peter 1:8-13

The Prayers of Paul

Paul recognized the importance of this type of knowledge and that's why in most of his prayers he never ceased demanding this knowledge. He is one of the outstanding writers who wrote a lot on this topic.

We conclude this chapter by recognizing and praying the same prayers that Paul prayed. Kenneth E. Hagin in his book *'The Believers Authority'* explained how he prayed these same prayers, and it brought a turnaround in his entire ministry. He prayed 2 - 3 times a day for about 6 months. He said, "I advanced more in spiritual growth and knowledge of the word in these six months than I had in the years as a minister and in more than sixteen years as a Christian. That was one of the greatest spiritual discoveries I ever made." *The Believers Authority* He prayed these prayers for others and for himself and he received tremendous results. His ministry was unquestionably outstanding; he stands today as one of the fathers of the faith movement. He brought the message of

187

faith to generations. His walk with God was marked by visible and authentic manifestations of epignosis.

I strongly believe that as you grow in Christ and as you desire this precise and correct knowledge of Christ, if you pray this prayer as Paul did with sincerity of heart, your life and calling will never be the same. We should be imitators of that which is good. What is written in the scripture is there for us to follow. If Paul prayed these prayers and they worked for him, they will work for you also. Personalize these verses and place your name there. Then pray it until you know you are in full possession of Epignosis.

"And this I pray, that your love may abound yet more and more in knowledge and in all judgment"

Philippians 1:9

"That the God of our Lord Jesus Christ, the Father of glory, may give to you the spirit of wisdom and revelation in the knowledge of

Him, the eyes of your understanding being enlightened; that you may know what is the hope of His calling, what are the riches of the glory of His inheritance in the saints, and what is the exceeding greatness of His power toward us who believe, according to the working of His mighty power"

Ephesians 1:17-19

"For this reason I bow my knees to the Father of our Lord Jesus Christ, from whom the whole family in heaven and earth is named, that He would grant you, according to the riches of His Glory, to be strengthened with might through His Spirit in the inner man, that Christ may dwell in your hearts through faith; that you, being rooted and grounded in love, may be able to comprehend with all the saints what is the width and length and depth and height— to know the love of Christ which passes knowledge; that you may be filled with all the fullness of God"

Ephesians 3:14-15 (NIV)

189

"I thank my God, making mention of you always in my prayers, hearing of your love and faith which you have toward the Lord Jesus and toward all the saints, that the sharing of your faith may become effective by the acknowledgment of every good thing which is in you in Christ Jesus. For we have great joy and consolation in your love, because the hearts of the saints have been refreshed by you, brother"

Philemon 1:4-7

Conclusion

Therefore we conclude this portion by saying that ginosko is what you know without any participation. It establishes a relationship with the object known. It is the complete package you received. Epiginosko is the continuation of the exploration of that package, oida is awareness and consciousness of it when explored, gnosis is your intellectual (soul realm) participation in it and epignosis is the end result where you become what you know, that's when you know as you are known. Proginosko speaks of the original plan and purpose of the Creator for you. It is the predestined life that Yahweh has bestowed upon us to fully explore and fulfilled, meanwhile gnostos refers to notable results and actions mostly found in the book of Acts. This gnostos encourages us to go for tangible results that bring transformation to our world. Let the world know of Yahweh and His mighty deeds in your life and the lives of others.

Therefore, beloved in the Lord, I urge you to bear fruit after having understood what epiginosko is; it is the fruit bearing process of your Christian walk. Do it with love and peace and you shall receive a greater reward and great grace shall be imparted to you. "... bringeth forth fruit as it doth also in you, since the day ye heard of it and knew(epiginosko) the grace of God in truth. "

Wisdom is the principal thing. You cannot have wisdom without knowledge. For wisdom is the application of knowledge. Now that you have acquired knowledge, go and apply it!

For wisdom will enter your heart and knowledge will be pleasant to your soul; Discretion will guard you, Understanding will watch over you

Proverbs 2:10-11

God bless you!

NB: We will be glad to receive your email regarding any suggestions, praise, testimonies critics or any information deem necessary. Shalom!

Notes

Notes

Made in the USA
Charleston, SC
20 April 2015